P9-CDQ-172

810.9
S977b

BROOK FARM

ITS MEMBERS, SCHOLARS, AND VISITORS

1 304

BY

LINDSAY SWIFT

New York

THE MACMILLAN COMPANY

LONDON: MACMILLAN & CO., Ltd.

1900

All rights reserved

COPYRIGHT, 1900,
BY THE MACMILLAN COMPANY.

Norwood Press
J. S. Cushing & Co. — Berwick & Smith
Norwood Mass. U.S.A.

PREFACE

It has often been said by those best qualified to know, and it may here properly be said again, that the veracious history of Brook Farm will never be written. Some of the most important records of its institutional life are hopelessly lost. Other material is lodged in the keeping of a former member, who has already made copious use of it. There are also before the world various recollections and memories of associates, scholars, and visitors once fully identified with this experiment. This literature of the subject is not inconsiderable, and much of it is entertaining and valuable; but it is often contradictory, often repetitious, and too often erroneous. No Brook Farmer of the first importance has chosen to write with fulness of his experience. The most which remains of the highest authority exists only in an occasional lecture, an agreeable paper of a personal nature, or some remembered conversation. Those to whom Brook Farm meant the most, have been the most silent, and its story was written — for only a few survive — deep in their hearts. This reticence did not find its reasons in sentiment alone. What is true of a movement like the Antislavery agitation is true also of Brook Farm. Both looked to the realization of a moral ideal, and the subtle spirit which animated both was perishable and incommunicable. It is more than fifty years since the last dweller in that pleasant domain turned his reluctant steps away from its noble illusions, and toward the stress of realities; but from no one of this gracious company has ever come the admission that Brook Farm was a failure.

There may yet be a place for a book which shall endeavor, without too much minuteness, to coördinate and present what really is known concerning the most romantic incident of New England Transcendentalism. There was a distinct beginning, a fairly coherent progress, but a vague termination. The enterprise faded, flickered, died down, and expired. Like some ill-contrived play, the Brook Farm Phalanx lingered during one more act, after the essential dramatic elements were exhausted. It is still possible to give a nearly complete account, and, it is to be trusted, without causing undue disturbance to the sensitiveness of the survivors or their friends, who, guarding the privacies and the arcana of what seemed to many a home life, would shield it from intrusion and vulgar disclosure. There has been no wish to make these pages a catch-basin for floating gossip or ill-natured anecdotes: these have been suffered to float, unstayed, out to the sea of oblivion. Manifest absurdities, the extravagance of youth, and the passing lights and shadows of the daily life may in fairness be considered as a relief to the seriousness of the story as a whole.

Inspired by a philosophical and speculative enthusiasm, Brook Farm began as an attempt to work modifications in social life. In this direct attempt it certainly ended in disaster. The visible fruits were intellectual, and of the men and women who contributed to the renown of Brook Farm as one of the true seeding-grounds of American letters it is the purpose of this book to speak, not critically or biographically, but rather from the personal side, and, in particular, as each person considered was affected by the associative life at Brook Farm. Some who came to a greater or less distinction were members, some scholars, and some were influential visitors.

It only remains to express my gratitude to Miss Mary Harris Rollins, who has rendered me the most loyal, friendly services and advice, and has herself renounced, to aid my own efforts, a long-cherished ambition to devote her ability and energy to a similar project.

I am indebted to all who have been approached with doubtless troublesome questions, for their unfailing kindness, and in particular to my mother, who permits me to print a hitherto unpublished letter from her former friend, Miss Georgianna Bruce, once a member of the Brook Farm Association. Many valuable data have been supplied by Mrs. Osborne Macdaniel of New York, once a resident of Brook Farm, and still mindful of its charm.

L. S.

AUGUST 11, 1899.

CONTENTS

BROOK FARM

ITS MEMBERS, SCHOLARS, AND VISITORS

BROOK FARM

CHAPTER I

THE TRANSCENDENTAL CLUB

THE distance seems wide between Immanuel Kant and the small group of social philosophers of the Transcendental Club in and about Boston fifty or more years ago; yet, but for him, and the schools of Fichte, Schelling, Hegel, and Schleiermacher, which immediately followed or schismatically differed from him, there would have been no Transcendental Club, and very likely no Brook Farm, although Kant might have recognized with difficulty the progeny of his own genius. "German philosophy" had powerfully affected two men in England: Coleridge, who especially felt the influence of Schelling even to the point of plagiarism, and Carlyle, who, best of his generation, interpreted German thought in both philosophy and literature. Coleridge derived his inspiration at first hand, for he lived and studied in Germany. With his extraordinary powers of absorption, he became so full of every sort of learning that

his genius overflowed upon other minds of his
generation, but he was not otherwise an originating force in his own country.   Carlyle
imbibed German philosophy mainly through
German literature.   Philosopher he never really
was, however vigorous a thinker and man of
letters.   He announced opinions and followed
convictions, but induction was often too slow a
method. (So far as he was inspirational and
given to intuitions, he remained a Transcendentalist,) in practice if not at heart, though the
name grew to offend him.   Emerson's calmness
and fairness made him tolerant of Carlyle's
later vicissitudes as the apostle of force and
hero-worship, but the real impression of the
more rugged genius on the gentler was made
while Carlyle was yet interpreting Germany to
England and America.

When Emerson introduced "Sartor Resartus" to America, a genuine interest in the best
of German thought was already fully under way
in this country.   Few as were the hands into
which the torch passed from Germany, through
England and to America, it is easy to underestimate the number.   Emerson takes pains to
attribute the beginning of the change toward
(individualism — and this, after all, is the real
form which Transcendentalism assumed in this
country)— to Edward Everett, and this beginning he sets at about the year 1820.   Everett

and George Ticknor both studied in Germany, and both brought home wholesome traditions of learning; neither of them was, however, outside the limits of a refined and earnest scholarship, fitted by character to promote or to lead a new movement in thought, although in their respective chairs at Harvard College, and through their finished and academic writings, they affected American literature. Emerson also includes Channing as one who brought fresh spiritual forces to combat the grim front of New England theology, adding that, "His cold temperament made him the most unprofitable companion." At the same time also there began to be studied in this country various forms and schools of French philosophy and social reform — late children of the first Revolution. Saint Simonism, the philosophy of Cousin, Joubert, Constant, Leroux, and presently the huge elaborations of Fourier, all made their way into temporary favor, in part as counteractions against the purer Transcendentalism, but particularly as directing attention to the need of political and social regeneration.

The scholars, — for it was at first an affair of scholars alone, — who were centred in Boston, were busied with this French philosophy, mainly eclectic, and were also inquiring deeply into German philosophy on their own account, though inspired by Coleridge, Carlyle, and by our own

pioneers to German universities. Particularly
were George Ripley, Margaret Fuller, W. H.
Channing, Convers Francis, Felton, James
Freeman Clarke — nor did these complete the
number — then looking into the original sources,
and not depending too much on the large claims
which Carlyle had begun to make as early as
1827 for his intellectual attachment to Germany.
Mrs. Dall, herself still living and a triumphant
apostle of the Newness, assigns to Frederic
Henry Hedge the leadership in this strong
movement of New England scholarship. Hedge
had been the private pupil of George Bancroft
here and in Germany, and his learning was of
the soundest; he was furthermore able to communicate his zeal to others. His influence was
no less potent, because all his life a certain envi-
able obscurity attended him, which enabled him to
build achievement, not reputation. It is of no
importance, however, who was first or last, greatest or least; the galaxy was small, but it was
brilliant, and each star helped to make it so.
The literary activity of the group was most
effectively shown in the series — the first of its
kind in America and edited by George Ripley
— entitled "Specimens of Foreign Standard
Literature," fourteen volumes in all, which began to appear in 1838. Miss Fuller, Felton,
Dwight, James Freeman Clarke, Samuel Osgood,
C. T. Brooks, and W. H. Channing contributed

to it. It was and still remains a creditable work, and some years ago it was republished in Edinburgh. There was by this means opened to a wider public a satisfactory approach to some of the names then influencing thought in France and Germany, and an interest was thus aroused here which had no parallel at the time in England.

Meanwhile other and native disturbances were taking place. The passing of a body of thought, in part directly from one country and in part through the medium of two others, might considerably sway a few minds, but would hardly affect any large mass of opinion, unless there were some internal dissatisfaction already at work; and this country, or that part of it then best representing its intelligence, was fully prepared for new gospels — a nidus ready for contagion. Unitarianism, having effectually divided the traditional church of New England, had already spread far beyond its early boundaries; and not destined to enjoy long, in its first integrity, the results of its wholesome accomplishments, had itself begun to fall apart. It was in the order of nature that the older Unitarians, who dared so boldly to sever from the parent stock, should themselves lament the departure of their own nurslings. Andrews Norton was not a man to let the Transcendentalists spread themselves like the green bay tree without strong protest. His "Latest Form of Infidelity" was the boldest, most defiant, and most arrogant attack which they were called upon to sustain. Puritanism was, and is to-day, as robust in a Unitarian as in a Trinitarian, provided only that he has the blood of the early saints in his veins; and Transcendentalism was a reaction against the essential conservatism of both the Unitarian and Trinitarian forms of Puritanism, neither of which cherished any belief in the self-sufficiency of the human mind outside of revelation. The Transcendentalists of Boston were not perhaps so anxious to domiciliate the philosophy of Kant, Cousin, and their congeners as to assert the supremacy of man himself and of each and every man as well.

Under such conditions, native and foreign, the Transcendental Club came into being in no sudden or violent way. In fact its development and realization were so natural that even to-day it is a matter of doubt if there ever really was such a club. The name, if accepted by the members at all, was taken as a necessity, not as a deliberate choice. Since all Boston insisted that certain people who used to meet occasionally made a Transcendental Club, there was no escaping the obligation. "I suppose," says Emerson, "all of them were surprised at this rumor of a school or sect, and certainly at the name of Transcendentalism, given nobody knows

by whom, or when it was first applied." Dr.
Hedge, writing forty years later, says that
Ripley, Emerson, George Putnam, and himself
called "the first meeting of what was named
in derision the Transcendental Club," but he
insists that this Club consisted only in occasional
meetings of like-minded men and women, and
that no line was drawn between those who
were members and those who were not, except
that due notification was always given to certain
persons. Those who were to be looked for at
such a coterie were Emerson, Alcott, Thoreau,
Stetson, the Ripleys and Mrs. Samuel Ripley,
Dwight, Miss Fuller and Miss Peabody, Parker,
Robert Bartlett, Jones Very, Convers Francis,
Weiss, Bartol, and Hedge. Now and again,
Bradford, Samuel Osgood, and Ephraim Peabody would come. Putnam, who found that the
meetings "took a turn unexpected to him," came
no more after the first meeting at Emerson's.
"Brownson," continues Hedge, "met with us once
or twice, but became unbearable, and was not
afterward invited." Of these choice souls, Dr.
Cyrus Augustus Bartol is alone living to-day
(1899), then one of the minor prophets, but
always a thorough Transcendentalist, though
after his own fashion, fearless, honest, and
not overweighted with discretion.

The Club was often called by the members
the Symposium, but the real name, if there was

any, was "Hedge's Club," inasmuch as a journey by him from Bangor to Boston insured a call for a meeting. The larger title, however, was foisted on these gatherings and was never repelled. Hedge has not been remembered so fully as he should have been in connection with the events of these few years; for he was an important factor, and was even asked to be an editor of the *Dial*, the most immediate result of the Club, when that periodical appeared in 1840. Among others identified with the Club were James Freeman Clarke, Thomas T. Stone, both the Channings, uncle and nephew, Samuel J. May, Samuel D. Robbins, C. P. Cranch, Hawthorne, George Bancroft, Clevenger, the sculptor, Dr. Charles T. Follen, Samuel G. Ward, William Russell, Caleb Stetson, Miss Sophia Peabody, who married Hawthorne in 1842, and Miss Marianne Ripley. Some of these were not members, yet all were within a fairly definite circle and followed a recognized cult. No trustworthy list of the members or meetings of the Club now exists. Though all shared to a greater or less extent the common fervor, and though discussion was as general as could be expected in such gatherings, the burden of talk and effort fell on the enthusiastic and willing few. It is understood that the first conference on September 8, 1836, considered the unhappy plight in which the Unitarian Church then found itself; and the preponderance in the Club of clergy, settled or unsettled, was so large, that the early discussions were naturally theological. Revelation, Inspiration, Providence, Law, Truth, and other generalities were treated openly and candidly. Not without truth was the charge then made that the main tendencies of the new spirit were toward Pantheism.

The occasional meetings went on with a singular amiability, until Ripley, always a leading voice, became so dissatisfied with his own attitude toward the office of the ministry that he resigned his charge late in 1840, and urged that some practical application should be made of the fresh views of philosophy and life. Emerson says that Dr. Channing took counsel with Ripley in the year of the latter's withdrawal from his Purchase Street pulpit "to the point whether it were possible to bring cultivated, thoughtful people together, and make a society that deserved the name." There is mention of a conference at the house of Dr. John C. Warren, which ended "with an oyster supper, crowned by excellent wines." Not too much in support of Ripley's project was to be expected of the Club itself; in fact, none of the original members accompanied Ripley to Brook Farm, and of the later members only Hawthorne and Dwight followed him; but they were all ready enough to listen to Alcott — and it was no unexacting

task — while he read Plato "as an equal"; their
features were composed and their minds attuned
to the Immensities and Eternities when this
discursive sage was asked "whether omnipo-
tence abnegated attribute." Indeed these Transcendentalists often found themselves enjoying
seraphic moods. Philosophy, foreign and domestic, was only a part of what they considered.
They were reformers in that they were dissatisfied with any ideal less exalted than their own,
and though far from a contentious or unamiable
set, they had the reformer's capacity for making
others feel a sense of ineptitude. The relative
fewness of their numbers made this unconscious
loftiness seem arrogance. But with all their tolerance of ideas, they had no ears for Ripley's
practical appeal. Emerson made the best known
refusal, and it was noble and honest; in replying
to Ripley's letter of November 9, 1840, he said
frankly that investments in Concord were se-
curer than they were likely to be at Brook
Farm. It was a favorite theory of Emerson
that method was unnecessary — a theory due
perhaps to a certain physical and mental inertness which the vulgar do not hesitate to call
laziness. In the *Dial*, in speaking of the young
men "who have been vexing society for these last
years with regenerative methods," he says that
they "all failed to see that the Reform of Reforms must be accomplished without means."

With the more cultivated and colder of the two sorts of Boston Transcendentalists this cheerful *petitio principii* found favor; but the younger and more radical, who said, according to Emerson, "I wish I was not I," were not satisfied. In this way Emerson and Ripley parted, one to his life of continuing serenity and to what in another would have proved a fattening optimism, and the other, with his little caravan, across the untried desert which lies between mankind and every Utopia.

Brook Farm was a Transcendental movement without doubt, but only, after all, in that it was a speculation of pure idealists, and that its inspiration came from the sources here so imperfectly outlined. The germ of Ripley's plan may have sprung from the "Neuhof" of Pestalozzi,— himself a genuine Transcendentalist, — concerning whom Ripley wrote an article for the *Christian Examiner* as early as 1832; or it may have been only one of the "private maggots" which Lowell, in his largest manner, said were then in everybody's brain. Whatever the remote cause, nothing short of some kind of realization of an ideal would satisfy Ripley. He had no doubt pottered long enough, though he had no unkind word to say, with the "intellectuals" of Boston. To understand properly the true parentage of Brook Farm, and especially the relations of the Transcendentalists to

reform, some pains must be taken to read contemporary opinions. The *Dial*, in particular,
was friendly to Transcendentalism and even
to Brook Farm, but the balanced nicety of its
good will is precisely typical of its passion for
individualism in opposition to association. In
the issue for January, 1843, Emerson boldly
asserts that there is no such thing as a Transcendental *party*, there is no pure Transcendentalist. He insists that it is Idealism — that
is, " Idealism as it exists in 1842 "; then follow
searching objections to the extravagance, the
separateness, the fastidiousness, and the inactiv-
ity of these friends of his bosom. But at the
close of this, one of his most coherent essays,
he finds use for all such by reason of their fineness
and discriminations. In a commendatory notice
of " An Essay on Transcendentalism " (Boston,
1842), an enthusiastic little book, the authorship
of which is attributed to Charles M. Ellis, son
of the previous owner of Brook Farm, the *Dial*
repudiates the notion that the new faith is re-
formatory ; " it has higher, nobler, lovelier work
than that of warring with the past or abusing
the present."

On the other side, Hecker, writing as late as
June, 1844, does not hesitate to say that " A
Transcendentalist is one who has keen sight but
little warmth of heart ; who has fine conceits,
but is destitute of the rich glow of love. He is

en rapport with the spiritual world, unconscious of the celestial one. He is all nerve and no blood — colorless. . . . He prefers talking about love to possessing it; as he prefers Socrates to Jesus. Nature is his church, and he is his own god." George Ripley, however, found no fault with the mental attitude of the Transcendentalists, but said that they desired "to reform the prevailing philosophy of the day," and that they relied on a faculty common to all men "to perceive spiritual truth when distinctly presented." It would be hard to find a closer explanation of the philosophy than that given by Nathaniel H. Whiting, a mechanic from South Marshfield, who, addressing a "Bible Convention," held in the Masonic Temple, Boston, on March 29, 1842, declared that "truths which pertain to the soul cannot be proved by any external testimony whatsoever." It was this sort of indoctrination among the supposedly unlettered which such men as Andrews Norton honestly feared, and which induced him to reprint in a pamphlet two all-important papers from the *Princeton Review*, written jointly by Drs. J. W. Alexander and A. B. Dod, both solid pillars of the Presbyterian Church. Dr. Dod took for his part an exposition of Cousin's philosophy, while Dr. Alexander arraigned the whole front of German transcendental philosophy. It was a sound and scholarly performance, and has furnished no little aid, even to Frothingham, and to those who have since studied this matter.

The plan of Brook Farm as a sociological experiment will not be dealt with here; nor will its relations with several communities which slightly touched its own life be especially examined. The essential difference between it and such other attempts at social reform as the Hopedale Community, the North American Phalanx at Red Bank, New Jersey, the Wisconsin or Ceresco Phalanx, and the Northampton Association of Education and Industry, was indicated by Charles Lane (*Dial* IV. 354), when he said of the West Roxbury Association: " It is not a community; it is not truly an association; it is merely an aggregation of persons, and lacks that oneness of spirit which is probably needful to make it of help and lasting value to mankind." The attempt to transform Brook Farm into a modified Fourierist Phalanx proved its ruin.

CHAPTER II

BROOK FARM

In the summer of 1840, Mr. and Mrs. Ripley boarded on a milk farm in West The Organization Roxbury. It was a pleasant place, varied in contour, with pine woods close at hand, the Charles River within easy distance. A close inspection of the substratum of sand and gravel would have confirmed a suspicion in the mind of a practical farmer that there was a reason why there had been no attempt to produce anything but milk on the estate; but the meadows, which formed a large part of the farm, were fair to see, and the fertile farms adjoining seemed to indicate a favorable soil and location. At all events, the Ripleys left it feeling that they had found a spot on which to carry out what had become their dearest wish: "to insure a more natural union between intellectual and manual labor than now exists; to combine the thinker and the worker, as far as possible, in the same individual; to guarantee the highest mental freedom, by providing all with labor adapted

15

to their tastes and talents, and securing to them the fruits of their industry; to do away with the necessity of menial services by opening the benefits of education and the profits of labor to all; and thus to prepare a society of liberal, intelligent, and cultivated persons, whose relations with each other would permit a more wholesome and simple life than can be led amidst the pressure of our competitive institutions." "To accomplish these objects," Ripley wrote to Emerson, in a letter of November 9, 1840, "we propose to take a small tract of land which, under skilful husbandry, uniting the garden and the farm, will be adequate to the subsistence of the families; and to connect with this a school or college, in which the most complete instruction shall be given, from the first rudiments to the highest culture."

When Ripley first talked over the subject of an association with Emerson, he thought that $50,000 would be necessary for its equipment; but at the time of writing the above letter he had decided that $30,000 would supply the land and buildings for ten families, and allow a sufficient margin to cover the first year's expenses. This sum he proposed to raise by forming a joint-stock company among those who were friendly to his enterprise, each subscriber to be guaranteed a fixed interest, and the subscriptions to be secured by the real estate. Ten thousand dollars of the amount he believed could be raised among those who were ready to lend their personal coöperation to the undertaking; the rest would be furnished by those whose sympathy could take only the form of financial encouragement. The shares he would place at $500 each; five per cent interest would be guaranteed, and the privilege of withdrawing would be allowed any shareholder who gave three months' notice of his intention. This last proviso, however, was modified when the Articles of Association came to be drawn up.

In the winter of 1840, Ripley decided to buy Brook Farm, making himself at first responsible for its management and success. About the first of April, 1841, he, with his wife and sister and some fifteen others, including Hawthorne, Mrs. Minot Pratt and children, George P. Bradford, and Warren Burton, took possession of the farm-house which, with a large barn, was already on the estate. The first six months were spent in "getting started," especially in the matter of the school, of which Miss Ripley was largely in charge, and it was not until the early fall — September 29 — that the "Brook Farm Institute of Agriculture and Education" was organized. By this time Minot Pratt and Charles Dana had arrived, and the Articles of Association were drawn up, the stock subscribed for, and the officers of the Institute elected. The signers of

c

the original agreement, in addition to the persons already named, were Samuel D. Robbins and Mary Robbins, his wife, David Mack, George C. Leach, and Lemuel Capen. Of these, Mr. and Mrs. Robbins and David Mack never allied themselves with the Association, Mack joining the Community at Northampton, which was organized in 1842. Twenty-four shares of stock were taken, and one-third of the amount was actually paid in, Mr. Ripley's library being his pledge for $400 of his subscription. These shares were distributed as follows: George Ripley held Nos. 1, 2, and 3, amounting to $1500; Minot Pratt, 4, 5, 6; William B. Allen, 7, 8, 9; Charles A. Dana, 10, 11, 12; Marianne Ripley, 13, 14, 15; Sophia Ripley, 16, 17; Nathaniel Hawthorne, 18, 19; Maria T. Pratt, 20, 21; Sarah F. Stearns, 22, 23; Charles O. Whitmore, 24. At the same time the following officers were elected: General Direction, — Ripley, Pratt, and Allen; Direction of Finance, — Hawthorne, Dana, and Allen; Direction of Agriculture, — Allen, Pratt, and Ripley; Direction of Education, — Sophia W. Ripley, Dana, and Marianne Ripley; Recording Secretary — Dana; Treasurer — Pratt. Allen, a young farmer from Vermont, had been engaged as head farmer for the first season, there being no other man of much agricultural experience in the company during the first few months, except Frank

Farley, who had previously spent some time at farming in the West. The vote "to transfer the Institution recently carried on by George Ripley to the Brook Farm Institute of Agriculture and Education from and after November 1, 1841," and "to transfer the establishment recently carried on by Marianne Ripley," was not passed until October 30, and was merely the formal ratification of earlier business transactions.

The farm was bought of Charles and Maria M. Ellis, and according to the deed, dated October 11, 1841, contained "about one hundred and seventy acres of land in that part of the town of Roxbury which has lately been set off from Newton," and on "the westerly side of the road leading from Dedham to Watertown." Another parcel of land, called the "Keith lot," lying on the opposite side of this road, was included in the same conveyance, but there is nothing in the deed showing the area of this lot, and it would be difficult, at this time, to establish its boundaries with any degree of certainty. The area was twenty-two acres. The consideration for the whole estate is stated to be $10,500. On the same day, October 11, 1841, Ripley, Hawthorne, Dana, and Allen, as trustees, mortgaged the property to Daniel Wilder and Josiah Quincy, commissioners of the sinking fund of the Western Railroad Corporation, to secure the payment of $6000 in three

years and twenty-one days; they also made a
second mortgage to secure to George R. Russell,
Henry P. Sturgis, and Francis G. Shaw the
payment of $1500 each, and to Lucy Cabot
the payment of $500. If the consideration
named in the deed from Ellis and his wife was
the real consideration (and it probably was), it
would seem that the trustees succeeded, at the
start, in mortgaging their property for $500
more than it cost them.

Each subscriber was entitled to the tuition of
one pupil for every share of stock held, instead
of his interest, or tuition to an amount not
exceeding twenty per cent interest on his investment. The consent of the trustees was
necessary to the legal transference of stock;
and any stockholder might withdraw his stock,
with the interest due thereon, by giving twelve
months' notice to the trustees. Every applicant
for resident membership was to be received
on a two months' probation, and at the end of
that time the established members were to de-
cide on his merits as a permanent acquisition, a
two-thirds vote being required for his admission.
It was agreed that labor should offset the price
of board — a year's labor for a year's board,
with lesser amounts in the same proportion.
Three hundred days' labor was to be considered
the equivalent of a year's labor and was to en-
title the Associate to one share of annual divi-

dend; sixty hours were to constitute a week's labor from May to October, inclusive; forty-eight hours, from November to April. The price of board to Associates who did not work was fixed at $4 a week — this to include rent, fuel, light, and washing. The children of Associates, over ten years of age, were to be charged half the regular rate; children under that age were to pay $3.50, "exclusive of washing and separate fire."

The Association was a joint-stock company, not incorporated. Every person who held one or more shares of stock was to be considered a member of the Association, and to be allowed one vote on matters relating to the disposition of its funds. The stock was non-assessable. The property was to be vested in and held by four trustees, chosen each year by the Association. The interest on the stock was to be paid in certificates of stock, although the subscriber was to be allowed, if he preferred, to draw on otherwise unappropriated funds the amount of interest credited in his favor; for no stockholder was to have any claim on the profits accruing to the Association beyond his guaranteed five per cent interest.

In view of the large results contemplated by this scheme, these preliminary articles seem very simple, and yet it was never felt that they were inadequate; for when the Association became later a collection of "groups and series," no change was made in the principles of its constitution, though the details were necessarily modified.

The course of financial events may be here conveniently followed to the end. In December, 1842, Hawthorne and Allen conveyed their interest as trustees to Ichabod Morton and John S. Brown; and on April 6, 1843, Morton's interest was conveyed to Minot Pratt. The two years which had then elapsed since the founding of the Association had not brought a sufficient number of new members to take up any large amount of stock, or to develop the farm and its industries to the point at which the income largely exceeded the outgo; and on the last mentioned date Ripley, Dana, Pratt, and Brown, as trustees, placed a third mortgage for $1000 on the property, which was taken by Theodore Parker, as guardian of George Colburn. This was payable on demand, and was to bear interest at five per cent; it increased the mortgage debts to $12,000. On October 7, 1844, Brown turned over his interest as trustee to Lewis K. Ryckman, and on May 3, 1845, the board of trustees, then consisting of Ripley, Dana, Pratt, and Ryckman, deeded the entire property to "a certain joint-stock company . . . incorporated by the General Court of the Commonwealth of Massachusetts by the name of the Brook Farm Phalanx, and . . . this day

. . . organized under the Act of Incorporation according to law." The Phalanx assumed the payment of all debts and obligations of every nature contracted by the former joint-stock company, and agreed to hold the trustees as well as all other agents harmless against all claims and documents contracted in behalf of the Association.

Three months later, August 20, 1845, the new corporation appears to have put on a fourth mortgage of $2500 to Francis G. Shaw, executed by "George Ripley, President of said Phalanx," and "Charles A. Dana, Chairman of the Council of Finance." The fact was so patent that the community must offer suitable accommodations for the families of desirable men who could aid in developing the industrial side of the experiment, that desperate measures seemed necessary to secure the completion of the partially constructed Phalanstery. Without doubt the Board of Direction felt that the increased productiveness of the farm, the new buildings and other improvements which they had achieved, warranted the placing of this last mortgage ; for although the financiering of the Brook Farmers may not have been adjudged able, it was never thought to be unscrupulous. The difficulties under which the leaders must have labored seem clear enough in the light of the facts disclosed by the Registry of Deeds of Norfolk County. Starting, apparently, with a capital of $4500 furnished by the paid-up stock and the balance between the cost of the farm and the amount raised by the first mortgage, a plant had to be provided with which to develop a wholly uncultivated soil and to set in motion the wheels of household industry. The insurance and interest on stock and mortgages were furthermore ever present problems.

The report of the Direction of Finance for 1842 and 1843 showed a deficit on November 1, 1843, of $1964.88; the report for 1844, a balance of $1160.84; and it seems to have been a matter of debate whether the last named sum should be distributed as dividends or allowed to go toward wiping out the preceding deficit; but it was finally recognized that the earlier loss might properly be considered as so much capital invested in permanent improvements on the estate, and that "the results of one year's industry ought to be divided irrespective of the results of former years, and certificates of stock issued to those persons who are entitled to such dividends." Later reports cannot be consulted, but the fourth mortgage sets aside any doubt regarding the general state of the treasury.

After the burning of the Phalanstery, which occurred March 3, 1846, it became far more difficult to raise capital or to dispose of stock. Since the structure had been built through investments on the loan stock, no insurance had been placed on the house, and the holders of partnership stock, therefore, and the regular members of the Association, had to bear the loss. About $7000 had already been laid out on the Phalanstery, and about $3000, it was estimated, was still needed. A current report, perhaps founded on a statement by Dana, that the insurance had expired the day before the fire, and that the failure to renew it had been owing to the carelessness of one of the Directors, does not agree with Ripley's own statement in the *Harbinger* of March 14, 1846.

For another year the quiet conflict went forward, and on March 4, 1847, at a meeting of stockholders and creditors, Mr. Ripley was "authorized to let the farm for one year from March 1, for $350; and the Keith lot for $100 or more, with such conditions and reservations" as he felt to be for the interests of the stockholders. At a later meeting of the stockholders, August 18, 1847, the President of the Phalanx was authorized "to transfer to a board of three trustees the whole property of the Corporation for the purpose and with power of disposing of it to the best advantage for all concerned." The board of trustees included Theodore Parker, George R. Russell and Samuel P. Teel.

On April 13, 1849, the farm was sold at public auction, and was bought for $19,150 by John L. Plummer, chairman of a special joint com-

mittee on the removal of the Roxbury almshouse.   On April 16, the Common Council of
the City of Roxbury instructed this committee
to acquire the estate.   Mortgages amounting
to $14,500, an execution in favor of Anna G.
Alvord, amounting to about $1961, and also an
accumulated interest amounting to $984 brought
the indebtedness of the Phalanx to $17,445.
The Phalanx, therefore, received $1704 toward
the settling of all other claims against it.   The
City of Roxbury established an almshouse on its
purchase.   In 1855 Brook Farm became the
property of the Rev. James Freeman Clarke,
who seems to have cherished a vague project
to colonize the place with desirable companions,
though the difference between his scheme and
an ordinary land speculation is not obvious.   In
1868 it passed into the hands of Lauranna C.
Munroe, who held it, as the wife of James W.
Munroe, until 1870.   The estate was then bought
by G. P. Burkhardt, who, shortly after, deeded it
to the "Association of the Evangelical Lutheran
Church for Works of Mercy," which to-day pro-
vides a shelter there for many homeless children in what is known as the Martin Luther
Orphan Home.

A seeker after country quiet and beauty
The Buildings might easily be as much attracted to-day by
and Grounds the undulating acres of Brook Farm as
were those who sought it as a refuge from so-

cial discouragement nearly sixty years ago. The brook still runs slenderly through the meadow; there are still the sunny uplands, the dim groves, and the denser woodlands; and human life still teems over it all. The farm-house which stood not far from the road when the life of the little community began, and which was naturally put to immediate use, was speedily christened the Hive. It was the heart of the community, though perhaps it would have been superseded had the Phalanstery reached completion. It was a house with two rooms on each side of a wide hall; those on one side were occupied by the vivacious Mrs. Barlow and her three sons, who came as boarders, and those on the other side served as sitting room and dining room, the kitchen being back of the latter. The upper rooms were used as sleeping rooms. With a growing family some reconstruction soon became necessary, and two of the rooms on the first floor were thrown together to make a larger dining room, which should also serve as an assembling place, not only for " Hiveites," but for the other residents; and both these needs it met so long as the community survived. Its ceiling was low; at each end of the room were two windows, and in the middle of one end was an old-fashioned fireplace of brick. There were as many as six long pine tables with benches on either side,

painted white; and the neatness and attractive-
ness of the apartment were emphasized by white
linen and white table-ware. The rooms on the
other side of the hall became parlor and office;
Mr. Ripley's library was arranged along either
side of the hall, and from a door at its farther
end one could step out into the meadow. To
the original building were added two wings containing rooms for laundry and other purposes,
with spaces for shed and carriage rooms under-
neath. There was a room, for example, where
mothers could leave their children in care of
the Nursery Group while they attended to their
daily work — a clear forerunner of the present
"day nursery." A large upper room in one of
the wings, occupied by single men, passed by
the name of Attica — a sounder jest than can
usually be found in the annals of Brook Farm.
Here, at one time, slept John Codman, the
General (Baldwin), the Parson (Capen), the
Admiral (Blake), and others.

The house faced toward the east, and was
separated from the brook and meadow below
by two terraced embankments enlivened by
shrubs and flower beds. Mulberry and spruce
trees gave character and background to these
adornments, and a great elm which stood near
the Hive and a sycamore which shaded it added
dignity to the ordinary looking dwelling.

New comers were wont to find their first welcome at the Hive, though one or two speak of arriving wholly unnoticed. There may have been a method in this silent absorption of a new member; possibly it was to convey the lesson at once of the unimportance of one individual more or less in the community. Whatever the reason, the conduct is noticeable. Mrs. Kirby says that when she arrived she found more than fifty persons assembled in the dining room. Miss Russell also speaks of this Trappist mode of reception. A swift impression for good or bad must have been formed on seeing so immediately the collected forces of the Association conducting themselves in their most unaffected manner.

To the south of the Hive was the barn, which also faced the east. Across the street from the entrance to the farm stood a small house which the community hired at first for the school, and which, except, perhaps, for one short interval, it retained for that purpose until the school was abandoned. This building, which was called the Nest, was in charge of Miss Ripley; here some of the teachers and pupils lodged. There was a feeling that the real life of the community was pent up within its own grounds, and that this section of the family without the walls, was to a certain degree isolated; and yet the records show no lack of participation by these individuals in the activities of the Association.

Early in 1842, the colony having outgrown
its accommodations, a house was built on
the highest point of land which the farm contained, a pudding-stone ledge forming the cellar
and two sides of the foundation wall. This
square wooden structure, in which the exterior
use of smooth matched boards served to produce
a most depressing effect, was so flimsily constructed that what went on in any one room
could be heard in every other room. It was
painted, after the imitative fancy of the day,
the color of gray sandstone. The only feature
which redeemed its severity was a deep, slightly
ornamented flat cornice which ran around the
top, although there were low French windows
through which one could step out upon the upper
of the two terraces. The house was reached by
a long flight of steps from the farm road. The
view was a delight; the Hive was distant about
three minutes' walk; there was a grove in the
rear, an orchard in front; and from some of the
upper windows might be had charming glimpses
of the river. Into this — the Eyrie, Aerie or
Eyry (as Mr. Ripley spelled it), Mr. and Mrs.
Ripley moved as soon as it was finished; Mr.
Ripley taking the greater part of his books with
him. The room on the right of the hall became
the library, but was also used as a recitation
room. In the parlor opposite was the piano, by
the aid of which John Dwight taught music, and

the family enjoyed many a rare evening. Behind these rooms were four small dormitories given over to pupils. Mr. and Mrs. Ripley occupied the room over the parlor, and Mrs. Kirby (then Miss Georgianna Bruce) and Miss Sarah Stearns were in the room behind them. Charles Newcomb and the Curtis brothers also roomed here, and Miss Dora Wilder was the housekeeper.

The Cottage — which alone of all the community buildings remains to-day — was the next house erected after the Eyrie. Mrs. A. G. Alvord, whose heart was in Brook Farm but whose health was precarious, built the Cottage, reserving a part for herself, but putting most of it at the service of active members. It was in the form of a Maltese cross, with four gables, the central space being taken by the staircase. It contained only about half a dozen rooms, and probably could not have accommodated more than that number of residents. Miss Russell says that it was the prettiest and best furnished house on the place; but an examination of the pathetic simplicity of its construction will confirm the memory of one of its occupants that contact with nature was admirably close and unaffected; from the rough dwelling, which resembled an inexpensive beach cottage, to outdoors was hardly a transition, and at all seasons the external and internal temperatures closely corresponded. The house was well placed on a clearly defined knoll, and the grass stretched directly from it in all directions except in the rear, where the flower garden had been started. The schoolrooms for the younger children were transferred to this building, and Miss Russell, Dwight, Dana, and Mrs. Alvord roomed here until the new organization was effected, when Miss Russell was moved to the Pilgrim House. The Cottage has always been known as the Margaret Fuller Cottage — although it was probably the only house on the estate in which Margaret Fuller never stayed during her occasional visits. It is one of the charms of a legend that its lack of truth only slightly detracts from the sentimental associations accumulated around it; and this is especially true of the Cottage, which still bears its traditionary honors. During a visitation of smallpox the Cottage was divested of its furnishings, and turned into a temporary hospital; and at another time it barely escaped entire demolition through the carelessness of some workmen who were digging a cellar under it. Until lately the Cottage wore its original dark brown color; and it is still the best visible remnant of the early days and gives a pleasant impression of what the daily life of the Association must have been.

The Pilgrim House was built by Ichabod Morton, of Plymouth, who planned to occupy it with his family, and who possibly hoped to persuade his brother Edwin to join him. It was a double house, placed south of the Cottage. There were double parlors, separated by folding doors, running across one end of the house, and two families might occupy these in common; a partition wall, built at right angles to the parlor, divided the rest of the building into two houses, each having its own entrance. Externally it looked like twin houses, back to back, and was a " very uncouth building." The barrenness of its appearance was the more marked because there were no trees about it; and standing, as it did, on high ground, it proclaimed, in its oblong shape and white paint, an austere New England origin. Ichabod Morton, after a brief residence of two weeks, returned to Plymouth, and the dwelling passed into the hands of the Association. The community took down the walls between the two kitchens, and thus provided a commodious and cheerful place for the laundry rooms; the tailoring department was established here, and here the *Harbinger*, the literary publication of Brook Farm, had its editorial office. The big parlor furnished a bare but convenient place for convivialities. Otherwise the dwelling was given over to lodging purposes.

In the spring of 1843 the construction of a

D

workshop was begun, according to Dr. Codman, some three hundred yards northwest of the Hive. It was a two-story building, sixty by forty, with a horse-mill in the cellar at first. This was later replaced by an engine which supplied power for the machinery used in the various branches of work. Partitions were put up as it became necessary to provide rooms for the different manufacturing industries which were introduced. The printing-office was placed on the second floor of the shop, and cot beds were sometimes set up on this floor for visitors who could not be cared for elsewhere.

Peter Kleinstrup, the gardener, probably arrived in the spring of 1843, and his coming gave a great impetus to the æsthetic consideration of the estate. A greenhouse was decided upon, and ornamental plants were cultivated during the outdoor season of that year, with the intention of placing them under cover in the winter. The fall came, but the money lagged, and at last a temporary shelter had to be provided in the sandy bank near the farm road. The project was by no means abandoned, however, and in the following spring fresh efforts were put forth in the direction of horticulture — partly as a business venture, and partly as an additional attraction to hoped-for members whose coming should hasten the days of prosperity. A garden, covering, perhaps, half an acre, was laid out behind the Cottage, with a chance of enlargement, if necessary, by cutting away some of the woods beyond. This land was carefully levelled and laid out with the walks and other precise accessories of a conventionally professional flower garden. In the fall of 1844 the gardener's heart was made glad by a building in which his treasures could be safely and conveniently cared for during the winter. The greenhouse was placed behind the Cottage and garden, near the boundary wall of the estate and parallel with it. To make room for the building, it was a painful necessity to plough up a beautiful patch of rhodora.

Nothing in the change to Fourierism showed more courage than the decision to accept the experiment with such modifications of the founder's scheme as were made necessary by restricted funds and fewness of numbers. There was some pretence of carrying out the theory of groups, and so far as was practical the main outlines were followed, but the great harmonic proportions of Fourier were simply out of the question. One feature, however, was clearly indispensable — a central house as laid down by the Master or Teacher, as Brisbane insisted on calling him. Accordingly, in the summer of 1844, the unitary building, or Phalanstery, was begun. It was placed in front of the Eyrie, at some distance from it, and nearly parallel

with the town road. All the public rooms
were to be in this building, which was almost in
the middle of the estate. The parlors, reading
room, reception rooms, general assembly hall,
dining room, capable of seating over three hundred people, kitchen and bakery, were carefully
planned for a common use. By the staircase
leading from the main hall — which was at the
left of the centre of the building — there was
access to a corridor-like piazza which extended
along the entire front of the house. From this
piazza opened seven doors leading to as many
suites, each containing a parlor and three bed-
rooms. The third floor was arranged in the
same way, and the attic was divided into single
rooms. The building was of wood and 175 feet
long. Thus the larger families, whose members
had been scattered by reason of the crowded
condition of the other houses, could be insured
a secluded family life, and such rooms in the
older buildings as were in use for other than
living purposes might be available for this legitimate need.

The work went on very slowly, however, and
by the time that it was necessary to stop work
for the season, only the foundation walls had
been laid and the first floor boarded. Some
progress was made during the spring and summer of 1845, but the hope of occupying the house
in the fall of that year had to be reluctantly aban-

doned. By the dawn of another spring, however, enough money had come in to stay the falling courage of the Directors. On Saturday, February 28, 1846, the carpenters put up a stove in the basement of the building, in order to dry it sufficiently to make work safe, and a fire was kindled there on Tuesday, March 3, in ignorance of a faultily constructed chimney. That night a dance was given at the Hive to celebrate what looked like the approaching fruition of hope; but the gayety was hardly well begun when the cry came that the Phalanstery was on fire. Treated at first as a joke, the gravity of the announcement speedily became evident, and the Associates rushed out to watch their own eclipse — complete and final.

The Phalanstery was not modelled closely after the unitary edifice of a Phalanx, and like other features of the change, was only a compromise with Fourier's original theories. It accorded, however, with the general plans of the Association, and great hopes were entertained of it. Except for the severe financial blow, Brook Farm had suffered no loss by reason of sentimental associations with the building, and the status was exactly as before. None of the usual functions were suspended, and every attempt was made to ignore, if possible, the seriousness of the situation. Minor dissensions were lulled by the common misfortune, and if bravery and

a common spirit of resolve could have raised
success from disaster, the fire might have proved
a blessing. When the excitement had passed,
however, there was a frank recognition of the
meaning of the calamity. Letters of sympathy
and some substantial assistance came, but there
was no evading the problems before the Association.

For once, at least, in its brief career, Brook
Farm was obliged to receive and acknowledge
gratefully the crude agency of a civilization
which it affected, playfully, no doubt, to de-
spise. The snow-covered ground threw back
the reflection of the blaze, and the glow was visible for miles. Aid came from all sides, and
" civilisées " worked to extinguish the flames, as
if the cause were sacred to themselves. The destruction, however, was soon complete, and there
was nothing left to do but to invite those who
had fought the fire to share the morning's breakfast, just ready from the baker's oven. While
these courtesies were going forward, George
Ripley thanked those who had helped him and
his associates. With that courage peculiarly
his own, — never so buoyant as during the hardest stress, — he assured the firemen that their
visit was so unexpected that he could only regret
that Brook Farm was not better prepared to
give them a " worthier if not a warmer reception." It is recorded that no one seems to have

labored more energetically to quell the flames
than neighbor Orange, who, though ironically
silent at festivities in the grove, gave his honest
strength in the hour of misfortune. He would
have little understood the submissiveness of
Dwight's sister, who wrote of the event: " I was
calm — felt that it was the work of Heaven and
was good." The sentimental character of some
of the members was brought out by the burning
of the Phalanstery, as it so often was by lesser
provocations, and an æsthetic appreciation of
the scene was not allowed to languish.

The Association had been in existence for
just five years. In that time it had built or
bought three houses, besides making substantial
additions to the original house; it had constructed a workshop and a greenhouse; it had
beautified and cultivated a large tract of land;
and it had nearly finished a huge Phalanstery,
seventy-five per cent of the cost of which
had been paid. In view of the small capital
with which the project started, this does not
seem a particularly meagre record of achievement.

The City of Roxbury had used the Hive for
an almshouse only about a year when it burned
down, the barn sharing its fate. The present
Lutheran Home was raised on part of the old
foundations of the Hive, and its printing-office
stands near by. The Eyrie and the Pilgrim

House have since fallen victims either to flames
or to weather; but the workshop is said to form
a part of the annex to the present Asylum. From
May 11 to July 8, 1861, the Second Massachusetts Infantry, under Colonel (afterward General) George H. Gordon, was quartered in what
was known as Camp Andrew, the camp occupying the slope now given over to the graveyard;
the regiment found on the estate a parade ground
large enough for the evolutions of a thousand
men — Brook Farm's best crop, according to the
mot of Dr. James Freeman Clarke, who was at
that time its owner.

The Industries   The industries relied upon to furnish
the visible profits of the Association were
many. It was expected that returns from these
sources would materially supplement the receipts
from new members who should come with property, from outsiders who should take up the stock
of the Association as an investment, and from
pupils and other boarders — the founders having placed their chief dependence on these
three means of revenue during the period of
development. How wide their expectations
shot of the mark, except in the case of the
school, has been brought out; and it remains
to show the strenuous attempts to make good
an income in other directions.

During the first two years little was undertaken beyond increasing the tillage of the farm

—a difficult and costly process. Although there was a large output of hay, it was not of a prime quality, and did not, therefore, bring high prices. Vegetables, fruit, and milk were marketable products, but much of the time the need of the Association itself for these articles was in excess of the supply. Dr. Codman is inclined to think that the time-limit of work in summer to ten hours, was unwise — that during the haying and harvesting season there were many days when it would have been an economy to disregard such a regulation; but this was one of the few cases in which Ripley sacrificed the future to the present.

In order to lay down new land, it was necessary either to plough up some of the grass land or to clear waste land of underbrush and bushes, and then to enrich it all to the point of productiveness. There were always two barriers which checked development along this line — want of men and want of manure. The farm could not supply the latter in sufficient quantities, and to buy liberally would have been beyond its purse. In dull seasons, it was considered prudent to dig muck, which, though serviceable, was not wholly satisfactory. When the nursery was decided upon, the community laid a heavy burden on itself, for, besides the cost of buying a multitude of young trees and seedlings, the necessary transplanting, budding, and grafting

had to be done by a man trained to the work.
For evident reasons, too, it was thought well to
keep the grounds in good order; and doubtless
this was indirectly a sound policy, although
circumstances conspired to make it ineffective.
The flower garden was perhaps the most dis-
heartening failure, for after a very careful preparation, it was found that the natural soil was
quite unsuited to the purpose, and that proper
fertilization was out of the question. The greenhouse, too, had not begun to pay its way when
the Association dissolved. It had required the
attention of two men, whose services might otherwise have been utilized in more profitable chan-
nels, and the fuel for winter added a large item
to the expense account. There is little doubt
that these things would have paid in the course
of time and that the embarrassment which the
Board of Direction suffered was attributable to
lack of capital rather than to lack of skill, although, in default of funds, more skill would
have enlivened the prospect. As it was, the
added fertility of the farm benefited only those
into whose possession it came later. Few
agricultural implements suitable for use on
such uneven ground were then obtainable, and
Dr. Codman asserts that not until the third or
fourth year was it thought prudent to buy a
horse-rake; this and a seed-drill, taken on trial,
were the only modern implements used. A

peat meadow, lying near the river, was one of the pleasantest spots in which to work, and several of the Associates were glad to turn in this direction when they could be spared from more pressing duties.

As the Community drew to itself a greater and greater variety of individuals, the trades at which they had previously worked were gradually introduced, until carpenters, printers, and shoemakers were at work, and the manufacture of Britannia ware and of doors, sashes, and blinds was established. The Shoe-making Group was of good size, consisting, probably, of eight or ten men in the latter days; but they were seldom overworked, although such sales as they made were fairly profitable. Britannia-ware lamps and coffee-pots did not find a ready market. The printers expended their time, for the most part, on the *Harbinger*, and the carpenters found ample employment on the estate. The sash and blind business ought to have been remunerative, for it was in the hands of George Hatch, an exceedingly capable man; but lack of capital was particularly disastrous to this industry. Lumber could not be bought in large quantities; furthermore, it could not be kept on hand long enough to become properly dried, and the vexation of customers whose doors shrank was great and justifiable. A formidable obstacle to prosperity was the distance of the farm from its market. It was nine miles from Boston and four from the nearest railroad station, now Forest Hills, and all the stock for manufacturing purposes, as well as family stores, coal, and manure, had to be transported by teams, while the manufactured goods and farm produce must go back over the same ground to be sold. This usually kept two wagons and two men on the road all the time, and diminished by just so much the productive strength of the Community.

The later organization of these industries under the Phalanx is outlined in the second constitution : "The department of Industry shall be managed in groups and series as far as is practicable, and shall consist of three primary series, to wit : Agricultural, Mechanical, and Domestic Industry. The chief of each group to be elected weekly, and the chief of each series once in two months by the members thereof, subject to the approval of the General Direction." "New groups and series may be formed from time to time for the prosecution of different and new branches of industry." A group consisted of three or more persons doing the same kind of work, although it seems not to have been permissible to use any but "harmonic numbers" in making up a group. Three, five, seven, or twelve people might combine to form a group, but not four, six, or eight. This was, of course, stark lunacy. In a Farming

Series of goodly proportions there would be a Planting Group, a Ploughing Group, a Hoeing Group, a Weeding Group, in the fields; a Cattle Group and a Milking Group, in the barn; a Nursery Group and a Greenhouse Group, in their usual places. The Mechanical Series included the manufacturing industries already named, and the Domestic Series was subdivided into Dormitory, Consistory, Kitchen, Washing, Ironing and Mending Groups. The Teaching Group was associated with no series; the commercial agents of the Association were detached personages, and so were the members of the "Sacred Legion," who volunteered to perform any peculiarly odious tasks. There was also a convenient Miscellaneous Group, the name of which indicated its duties.

Great stress was laid on the interchangeableness of these occupations. If a carpenter's work was slack, or he was temporarily weary of carpentering, he could exchange his plane for a scythe, or a hoe, or a milk-pail at any time. This presupposed an unwonted versatility, which was more likely to show itself within the groups of the Domestic Series than elsewhere. The "chief" of each group kept a carefully tabulated account of the work done by each member of his group, regular or "visiting," and at the end of the season it was possible to make accurate returns of the number of hours applied to

the prosecution of each industry. Mr. Ripley
was of the opinion that this arrangement secured "more personal freedom and a wider
sphere for its exercise;" and that there was "a
more constant demand for the exercise of all the
faculties." It is possible that the waste of time
which was incurred by this system was offset by
the waste of nervous energy which is undoubtedly occasioned by the friction of competitive
life. George Bradford has said that many
hours were lost through lack of any definite
school programme; for it frequently happened
that a teacher who was digging on the farm
would leave his work to meet an engagement
with a pupil; but the pupil, being absorbed in
the pursuit of woodchucks, would either forget
his appointment altogether, or put in an appearance an hour late. It is also plain that undue
time and prominence was given to the matter of
elections. Each group was to elect a "chief"
every week, and once in two months all the
"chiefs" of the same series were to meet and
choose a "chief" for that series. This was
only one of the badges of mental vulgarity
which Fourierism wore. It left out of the
account all questions of fitness for leadership,
and dwelt on the baser desire for notoriety or
conspicuousness as opposed to merit. It may
have been a preventive of jealousy, although
that is doubtful. Indeed, since Fourierism

made a ritual of organization, only limited minds could accept it for any length of time.

The Transcendental Brethren of the Common Life had it well in mind not only to think together, though not certainly alike, to drudge with a holy and equal zeal, no matter how humble or how high the diverse tasks, but to give the theory of Association the sharp test of a communal table and to elevate domestic service to noble conditions. If, during the years of trial, there were grumblings over necessary economies of fare, there was hardly a note of shirking or dissatisfaction among those who humbly yet proudly served. " Nathaniel Hawthorne, Ploughman," in his first enthusiasm wrote to his sister: " The whole fraternity eat together, and such a delectable way of life has never been seen on earth since the days of the early Christians. We get up at half-past six, dine at half-past twelve, and go to bed at nine." This seraphic content died soon in the heart of the romantic ploughman, but the health and joy born of simple food and unpretending equality satisfied the Brook Farmers so well that they varied little the household plan with which they began. " Our food was very plain, but good," says Miss Russell; but she adds that fresh meat was not always to be had. On Sundays, beans and pork were furnished, not only in accordance with local tradition, but also

The House-
hold Work

as a luxury befitting the day and in recognition of that occasional orgy which a latter day English Socialist holds to be a necessity of human life. Pandowdy is mentioned by one writer as a delicacy, while Miss Russell speaks with feeling of brewis — a dish now passing into undeserved neglect, but once in New England of great repute. Temperance in food was the rule; in regard to drink, it was a matter of principle. The close union of the school and the Association would have invited hostility toward even the most restricted use of wine, beer, or spirits. When the evil days began, there was retrenchment in the cost of living as in other ways. The use of coffee was modified, and the quality of butter noticeably fell. Such details speedily aroused the attention of outsiders, but there is evidence that the Brook Farmers took their hardships in the same buoyant spirit in which they entered the experiment as a whole.

Radical in many ways these reformers certainly were; they often contravened social habits, and roused unfeigned astonishment and amusement in persons of discretion and solid worth. But they were not Bohemians, and had few of the proclivities of that agreeable and undeterminable fellowship. Even tobacco, that constant solacement to those at odds with respectability, was in little vogue. One woman says that this indulgence was held in such contempt by the socially dominant sex that no man essayed the practice of it; but there were at least three smokers — Baldwin, Pallisse, the engineer, and Kleinstrup, the gardener, whose vain efforts to abjure his shame have been sympathetically pictured by a fellow worker.

Simple as the dietary was, there were in this hive of oddities some who went even yet further from the world's ways of eating. There was a Graham table, at which sat vegetarians, who were for eating no flesh while the world stood, and who even denied themselves tea and coffee. It was an era of cold water and unbolted flour. It was not so much a question what to eat as what not to eat. Emerson, it is remembered, decided not to invite Charles Lane to sit at his Thanksgiving board lest that over-principled copartner of Alcott should make an occasion for ethical improvement over the turkey. The vegetarians had a fair chance at Brook Farm to test the comparative value of their faith; and it is known that they stood well with their associates for endurance, persistence, and general good health. This relatively equal footing may, however, have been due to the involuntary continence of those who chose a wider but at best a very unpretentious menu. It has been said that it was the custom to put a cent down by one's plate for each cup of tea ordered;

E

but whether the rule held for all, or only for visitors, it is not possible to say.

The usual duties were mainly discharged by the young women, no attempt being made to foist on the men tasks beyond their experience or knowledge. As volunteers and gallant aids to the household brigade the men were, however, welcome, and made themselves useful and possibly attractive. They were of special service in the laundry, where the pounding, wringing, and hanging out of clothes was a severe test of muscular strength, since there were no mechanical adjuncts to this department. Appliances to reduce the irksomeness of the trivial round were few; a pump was the main dependence for water, and duly appointed carriers visited daily each house and supplied the empty pitchers, sometimes attended, in stormy weather, by a youth who carried an umbrella. Curtis occasionally trimmed lamps, and Dana organized a band of griddle-cake servitors composed of "four of the most elegant youths of the Community." One legend, which has the air of probability, deposes that a student confessed his passion while helping his sweetheart at the sink. On washing-day evenings offers of help in folding the clothes were never rejected, and the work went fast and gayly. Similar gatherings prepared vegetables for the market in the barn on summer evenings; and while chivalry and the ardor of youth went far toward lightening these household tasks, the young men had to exert themselves to hold an even pace with the sex permanently skilled in deftness. The excess of young men in point of numbers over the young women is partly responsible for their large share in these domestic labors, and a desire to free the young women for participation in some further scheme of entertainment was not seldom a motive power. It would be too much to expect that this ecstatic fervor should be constantly maintained, but during the earlier years the men certainly discharged well and with commendable patience their moiety.

Visitors were amused at the "fanaticism exhibited by well-bred women scrubbing floors and scraping plates, and of scholars and gentlemen hoeing potatoes and cleaning out stables, and particularly at the general air of cheerful engrossment apparent throughout." Monotony there must have been, and often, but it is the testimony of all who have spoken, that the real marvel was that so much variety and good spirits were introduced. Little sympathy was needed for the well-bred women and the scholars, because as soon as was practicable, special capacity was developed and youthful training for particular service was made available. Miss Russell says, "I was early taught to clear starch," and "offered to make up the muslins of all on the place who wore them." Muslins were certainly a luxury from a communal point of view, and perhaps, like other futilities and unnecessary details, were not encouraged. There were no curtains, and no carpets except on one or two of the "best rooms."

In the beginning there had been a hired cook, but when economy became imperative, one of the women associates offered to undertake this trying duty, and in spite of unsmothered growling over her efforts at retrenchment, she adhered to her chosen post and to her policy *usque ad finem*. Peter Baldwin — the "General" — filled the important rôle of baker, thus reducing to a minimum the demands upon the cook.

Emerson, who never refers to Brook Farm without conveying to the finest sense the assurance that some one is laughing behind the shrubbery, notes the disintegrating tendency of these harmonious souls, when he says: "The country members naturally were surprised to observe that one man ploughed all day, and one looked out of the window all day — and perhaps drew his picture, and both received at night the same wages."

At its fullest, life there had few complexities, but it strove to spread beyond the bounds of the few acres of the farm. Some of the women saw possibilities of introducing leaven into the eventless farm life of the near neighborhood, and of showing the good wives about them that the commonplaces of milking, churning, and the preparation of coarse fare could become glorious by the gospel of Brook Farm. Alarmed already at neighbor Orange's innate fondness for butchering, and wishing to spread softening influences, two Sisters of the Transcendental charity called on the family of a farmer hard by "whose spirit level was soft-soap, rag mats, tallow-dips, and patch-work quilts." Defeat was swift and inevitable, and a decision was born of the futile experiment that women's time is largely wasted in unprofitable "social life."

The amelioration of the human lot was not the only quest; if it was not possible to indoctrinate farmers' wives, there were still left the dumb beasts, conservative to be sure, but docile and perhaps open to conviction. Domestic hygiene met with a sharp rebuff when a plan to raise calves on hay-tea was set in operation. This attempt to dispense with the maternal office of the cow proved fatal to the particular calf selected for the experiment. Ripley is said to have worn an air of ill-concealed guilt during the decline and fall of this well-intentioned theory.

Enjoyment was almost from the first The Amusements and Customs a serious pursuit of the community. It formed a part of the curriculum and was a daily habit of life. The few disaffected individuals who held aloof threw no continuing

chill on the main body of youth and good spirits,
though one may suppose that Charles Newcomb,
who played successfully at æsthetic Catholicism,
was something of a blight at times, and that
the occasional appearance of the contentious
Brownson was no signal for mirth. Emerson
has given the lasting impression that Brook
Farm was a continuous *fête champêtre ;* he has
even stated specifically that as the men danced
in the evening, clothespins dropped from their
pockets. Legendary as this no doubt is, it ex-
presses well the outsider's conviction that merriment reigned at Brook Farm.

The wholesomeness of the life has never been
seriously called in question, and nothing bears
weightier testimony to its sanity than the simple
and spontaneous character of the sports which
found acceptance. Out-of-door life was a passion which, like all noble passions, absorbed into
itself many less worthy emotions, and lifted very
ordinary amusements out of the sphere of the
commonplace. Even the uncommendable habit
of punning, by which the entire community, led
by the arch-punster Ripley, was at times infected, may perhaps be explained as one of the
forms of effervescence induced by superabun-
dant oxygen.

After meals, in the evening, and when it was
possible to be in the open air, the Associates
made happiness a duty, and their high courage

held them to harmless fun when fainter souls
would have drooped at the whisperings of evil
days ahead. Except in the dead of winter, the varied acres of the domain itself, as well as the
surrounding country, served as a setting for the
animation which the finished labors of the day
had set free, and the younger members of the
family, especially, walked and picnicked through
the outlying regions; the great boulders forming " Eliot's pulpit " invited strolling feet; there
were junketings at Cow Island, boating parties
on the Charles River, the beauties of which at
and near this part of its course have never had
their deserts; and expeditions were made even
to the distant woods surrounding Muddy (now
Turtle) Pond, which at that time were felt to be
full of mysterious dangers, but which now offer
an uninteresting security through the efforts of
a paternal state commission.

Sundays were naturally most favorable for
the quieter of these amiable strayings, but church-
going was not neglected. Some of the members
would go to West Roxbury to hear Parker, while
others of more persistent faith and sturdier legs
would push on to Boston, where lay a larger field
of choice for their unprejudiced tastes. Hawthorne has given the most charming descriptions
of the places to be reached by walking, but inasmuch as his expeditions were taken on his own
account, they lack the humanizing significance

which those of the wandering groups of less
seclusive members seemed to have.

Although there would be, now and then, during the winter, a "fancy party," the true revels
of this sort were reserved for warm weather, and
were held in the still beautiful grove. Dancing
was much in vogue, and was enjoyed by all who
knew the art. Dr. Codman tells with conscious
pride that he has seen five men who had been
trained for the ministry engaged in this courtly
pastime at one time. The fashion was to dispose of the supper dishes with astonishing rap-
idity, and then to clear the dining hall for the
evening's pleasure. Youth was at the prow, as
usual, but the elders were not discountenanced.
Towering above the rest was the figure of "the
General" (Baldwin) displaying more vigor than
grace, but not less welcome because the room
seemed smaller by his presence. Often the
dance was less formal even than this, and consisted of half a dozen of the younger people
who strolled into the Cottage after supper and
took turns as players and dancers for an hour
or so, dispersing, at the end of that time, to the
real call of the evening.

If dancing was the froth of their life, conversation was the substance. Dr. Codman says
Brook Farm was "rich in cheerful buzz." The
talk ran from the heavy polemics, fortunately occasional, of Brownson, and the cheerful impetu-

osity of the high-souled Channing, down to the thinnest sort of punning. To revile this manner of jesting is almost as commonplace as to indulge the practice itself; but if we may trust to friendly memories, the habit was really a feature of the intellectual life. The certainty that the custom was rife would help to establish an impression that some high intelligences are devoid of nice perceptions of wit, as it is evident that they often lack the faintest relish for music or art. To have been present at one of these joyous gatherings, and to have heard the gay sallies, would have softened the hardest objector; but little thanks are due the painful diarists who have embalmed the persiflage in such a way as to remind one of that sorry humor at the *pension* in Balzac's "Père Goriot." Another frank touch of mediocrity was the constant iteration of phrases. For a long time, after one of Mr. Alcott's visits, a pie was always cut "from the centre to the periphery"; and Mrs. Howe avers that a customary formula at table was: "Is the butter within the sphere of your influence?" Mrs. Ripley declared herself at one time weary of "the extravagant moods of the young girls," and "sick of the very word 'affinity.'" "Morbid familism" was a frequent reproach brought against exoteric civilization. But extravagance was a mood of the era and not of the place. A striking instance of this

excess occurs in an article on Woman, signed
"V." and printed in the *Present:* "Throw your
libraries into the streets and sewers on the
instant that you find, as you will, all knowledge
within yourselves."

In stormy weather a favorite diversion was
an impromptu discussion in the Hive parlor.
Several subjects were proposed, a vote was
taken, and the choice of the majority decided
the question to be debated. There is an account by Mrs. Kirby of a well-sustained argument on the query: "Is labor in itself ideal, or,
being unattractive in character, do we, in effect,
clothe it with the spirit we bring to it?"

The winter amusements were varied. Skating
took the place of boating, and proved especially
alluring to those of Southern birth. Sometimes
a party, including the children and elders as
well as the young men and women, would visit
the river with sleds and skates, and maturity
and youth would run a very even race for the
prize of pleasure. Coasting was not neglected,
although the opportunities for its indulgence
were meagre. One of the few accidents which
have been thought serious enough to be remembered resulted from one of these revels.

There was naturally much in-door recreation
during the winter. Literary societies and reading clubs flourished; Shakespeare received due
attention, and the readings in connection with

the study accorded him were enlivened by occasional happenings not recorded in the text, as
in the case of a failure of one of the best readers
to give a satisfactory rendering of Romeo for
the inartistic reason that the Juliet did not suit
his taste.   Cornelia Hall, who boarded for
periods of varying length at the Farm, used
to give remarkable dramatic readings, which
attracted attention from the outside world.
Father Taylor esteemed it a high privilege to
go out to hear her read the " Ancient Mariner."
On Sunday afternoons, during the earlier years,
Ripley elucidated Kant and Spinoza to those
who cared to listen, and there were often lectures by such gifted friends of the community
as Emerson, Margaret Fuller, Alcott, Brisbane,
and Channing. George Bradford and Mrs. Ripley were members of a class which read, without an instructor, the greater part of Dante's
" Divina Commedia " in the original, the students reading aloud in turn.   In summer this
coterie held its meetings out of doors.   No serious intellectual work engaged the community
as such, even in its first freshness ; most of the
people were too young, life was too radiant, and
the daily routine was sufficiently exhausting to
make the hours of recreation welcome.   A con-
sociation of mental effort could hardly expect to
accomplish the highest results — these are for
the lonely and strenuous individual.

Impromptu tableaux, dialogues, and charades were in good repute, but the best talent of the Association found expression in an occasional play, sometimes of the most ambitious character. Good material for acting existed, although no one in later life seems to have developed his or her capacities in the direction of the stage. Whenever an elaborate dramatic entertainment was taken in hand by the Amusement Group, the lower floor of the workshop was called into service in place of the Hive dining room. In the shop, Chiswell, one of the carpenters, had built a portable stage which could be set up for rehearsals and removed afterward with very little trouble. Dr. Codman gives an account of the attempt instigated by John Glover Drew, an ardent admirer of Byron, to produce scenes from the " Corsair "— an effort which the community and the visitors from the neighboring village frankly set down as a melancholy failure. Sheridan's " Pizarro," too, was undertaken, and much merriment was caused by Rolla's fall under a shot which was fired several minutes after he had been disabled by it. The visitors, including Parker, on this occasion, gently withdrew long before the play was over, and the Associates had the good sense to accept this courteous hint that they were not at their best in this field of histrionics.

Card-playing never seems to have kindled a

wide interest, though Codman speaks of "con-
chas and euchre," for which Baldwin had a passion. A story is extant of a "Hive" youth who
was discovered by Dana, a firm disciplinarian,
playing whist at the Cottage after ten o'clock
(the hour at which the pupils were expected to
be in their own rooms). "And how do you expect,
sir, to enter the house, when you know the
doors are locked at ten?" "Oh, I always get
in at the pantry window!" This "early
closing" regulation was apparently hard and
fast; but on two occasions it was broken,— at one
fancy ball, and at one of Brisbane's lectures.

Music there was at all times. Some of the
Associates had good voices, and musical visitors
were common. To have heard those splendid
youths, George and Burrill Curtis, sing the "Erl-
King" was something to recall with tenderness.
The younger brother had a way of amputating
the weak or silly words from some old tune, to
which he would then add good modern poetry
with delightful effect. Two charming women,
Mary Bullard and Frances Ostinelli, came to be
well known at the Farm, and their graceful
compliance with requests for their songs has
been gratefully remembered. Frances Ostinelli,
better known as Signora Biscaccianti, appeared
during the first summer after the change. She
was then seventeen years old, and possessed a
voice of unusual sweetness and strength. It is

said that people living on Spring Street in West
Roxbury, three-quarters of a mile away, could
hear her singing in the open air. When
Christopher Cranch came, the young people
were full of glee, for they knew that he could
provide many varieties of entertainment, musical and literary. Miss Graupner's piano-playing,
too, was heartily sanctioned, and the occasional
quartettes which Mr. Dwight imported from
Boston gave deep satisfaction. The Hutchinson
family, consecrated to the cause of antislavery
and temperance, but naturally interested in other
phases of social reform, drifted in time to Brook
Farm, where everybody was moved by their perfect singing of indifferent music, which probably
seemed less than mediocre to ears and tastes
which had been trained by John Dwight. Abby
Hutchinson, whose name is a synonym to most
of us for a scarlet velvet bodice, was only
thirteen at this time, and here as everywhere
was the centre of much sympathetic interest.
This famous group of radicals went forth from
their visit much refreshed by what they found,
and even sought to turn their own home at
Milford, New Hampshire, into a miniature
Brook Farm.

Partly from necessity, partly from choice, it
was customary for the young people to sit on
the floor or on the stairs during evening enter-
tainments at the Eyrie, and the habit produced

a variety of comments : George Bradford thought it very pretty; Margaret Fuller found it very annoying. When the washing and wiping of dishes was going on, often the group employed would ease the task by singing "O Canaan, bright Canaan," or "If you get there before I do," or some other secularly religious song, dear to the "Elder Knapp" period. Attendance at concerts and lectures away from the Farm was comparatively of infrequent occurrence; there was so much that was interesting, absorbing, and high in quality at home, that there was no particular inducement to seek diversion abroad. Whenever such excursions were taken, the motive was usually something more serious than a search for pleasure. Nothing better evinces the fine zeal of these Brook Farmers — some of them simple folk enough — than their journeying to Boston to hear good music, and then walking back a good nine miles under the stars and in the middle of the night, with an early morning's work before them. This same warm interest attached to the Associationist meetings in Boston in which Mr. Ripley usually took a leading part. Antislavery gatherings in Boston and Dedham were attended by large numbers who went in farm wagons. Only one or two of the Association were zealously committed to this cause, but it would have been impossible for so humane a company to remain untouched by the

call for sympathy which was sent up all about
them. One woman (Mrs. Leach ?) was so deeply
imbued with antislavery feeling that she dis-
carded the use of the linen collar until the slave
should be paid for his work. It is not quite
certain whether she confounded cotton with
flax; but her reasoning was less direct than
that of Charles Lane, who decided that linen
was the only fabric which a moral man could
conscientiously wear. The use of cotton, he
held, must certainly be discouraged because it
gave excuse for the employment of slave labor;
and he further argued that in our choice of
wool for clothing we rob the sheep of his natural defences. Another Brook Farmer, a woman,
scoffed at amenities of clothing by quoting : —

"And the garment in which she shines
        Was woven of many sins ; "

but as regards dress the majority of the family,
while they sought first comfort and suitability,
had a normal regard for the beautiful and artis-
tic. When about their work the women wore a
short skirt with knickerbockers of the same material; but when the daily tasks were ended,
they attired themselves after the simpler of prevailing fashions. There was a fancy for flowing
hair and broad hats; and at the Hive dances
there might be seen wreaths woven from some

of the delicate wild vines and berries found in the woods, twined in waving locks.

It is said that the motive of economy was responsible for the adoption, by the men, of the tunic in place of the "old-world coat." This favorite garment was sometimes of brown holland, but often blue, and was held in place by a black belt; and for great festivals some of the more fortunate youths possessed black velvet tunics. Such an unusual article of raiment excited as much dismay in the outer world as the idiosyncrasies of other reformers, and has been described as a compromise between the blouse of a Paris workman and the peignoir of a possible sister. Colonel Higginson speaks of the "picturesque little vizorless caps" worn by the young men as being "exquisitely unfitted for horny-handed tillers of the soil." Economy of labor may have been accountable for the unshorn face, but the beard was certainly in high favor at Brook Farm, and a predilection for long hair was also current. One of the residents, probably Burrill Curtis, who had been a model for a portrait of Christ, is described by Mrs. Kirby as a "charming feature in the landscape," while the quality of his temper was attested by the serenity which he showed when stoned by some boys on a pier for daring to leave his hair unclipped in the presence of wharf rats and other good tories.

F

Miss Russell was at first conscious of a sense of the ludicrousness of the place, but found that this soon wore away; on the whole, excepting always the jejune effect of over-enthusiasm, there was singularly little display of bad or inaccurate taste. There may have been exaggerations, but there was no loudness. The radicalism of the Farm was as little offensive as that of Edmund Quincy and Samuel Sewall in their sympathy with the antislavery movement. It tended toward beauty in appearance, action, and thought. The pose of arrogance toward "civilisées" betrayed a slight lack of humor — a common deficiency in reformers — and a little dulness of perception; but the balance of good manners was restored by a more considerate tone toward the socially less favored. A theoretical equality never seems to have entered anybody's head.

"The symbol of universal unity" was made on a number of solemn occasions, — as at John Orvis's marriage to Marianne Dwight, and at the close of one of Channing's sermons in the grove. The entire company would rise, join hands, thus forming a circle, and vow truth to the cause of God and humanity. One such outpouring of emotional sincerity, which occurred after four years of community life, attests the solid basis of an expression of feeling which earlier might have seemed hysterical.

It is always to the credit of a reformer that he is willing to look into schemes proposed by other reformers, and Brook Farm was liberality itself toward new ideas outside its own field. The water-cure and the starving-cure both received due attention at the hands of some of the members of the household. Mrs. Kirby's account of the treatment at a cold-water cure a few miles from Brook Farm is vivid, but not alluring. Thirteen barrels of ice-cold water were yielded up daily by a natural spring, and this supply was dammed until a patient was ready for it. Then the sluices were opened and the water allowed to pour down an inclined plane and fall a distance of twenty-five feet upon the back of the shuddering victim. The sensation is said to have been that of pounding by glass balls. "Umschlag," or wet bandaging, was a treatment reserved for the following day. Strict prohibition was put on visits to the Farm in the intervals between douches, for the reason that all excitement must be avoided, in order that the cure might be efficient. The starving-cure had an ardent follower in a young Hungarian, Count G—— (possibly Gurowski though not probably), who, for a time, shared the fortunes of the Farm ; but the simple menu of the community removed any pressing need for the general application of this treatment.

Of sport, in the restricted and technical sense,

there is no record. People who felt doubts of
the moral character of their butcher, simply because he was a butcher, could not take kindly
to hunting, and probably not even to fishing.
Dr. Codman says : " I do not remember ever
seeing a gun on the place ; " and the chances
are that the woods about the Farm and the
quiet waters of the Charles held undisturbed the
life within them.

CHAPTER III

THE most immediate and at times the only source of income was the school, the establishment and maintenance of which always held a conspicuous place in this scheme. The transcendental philosophy could not well avoid laying particular stress on intellectual development and culture, and the student life of the farm was animated by a pervasive enthusiasm and held to an unvarying standard. In certain particulars the educational policy was ideally good, proceeding as it did on the theory that perfect freedom of intercourse between students and a teaching body of men and women whose moral attainments were not distanced by their mental accomplishments, could not fail to justify itself. During the first two years the chief disciplinary measures consisted in the attempt to arouse a sense of personal responsibility, and to communicate a passion for intellectual work. There were no study-hours. Each pupil studied when and where he would, and recitations for the older students were distributed through the latter part of the day.

The farm was always short of "hands," but there was never any lack of heads in the Department of Instruction — an incidental testimony to the superiority of the Association's brain power as compared with its muscular ability. There was an infant school for children under six; a primary school for those under ten; and children whose purpose it was to take the regular course of study laid down by the institution were placed in the preparatory school, which fitted youths for college in six years. Otherwise the studies were elective. There was also a course in theoretical and practical agriculture, which covered three years, and which was in charge of John S. Brown. It was understood that each pupil should give an hour or two each day to some form of manual labor — a requirement that met with disfavor from some, at first; but resentment quickly gave place to interest, if not to devotion, and an outsider usually found it impossible to distinguish between the members and the pupils of the Association in the matter of attachment to the cause. One of the commonest avocations for the boys was hoeing, and the girls helped at dish-washing and other of the lighter household tasks. Much stress is laid on the quality of the class-room work in consequence of the wholesome physical condition produced by this unique environment. On the other hand, it is not to be denied that some of the pupils who worked eight or ten hours a day, as an equivalent for board and instruction, and studied hard besides, met with the usual fate of those who ignore physiological laws. Much of the boisterousness of youth was lacking; partly because many of the usual artificial conditions against which boisterousness is a natural protest were absent, and partly because all but the youngest realized something of the seriousness of the purpose which underlay the undertaking. Laughter and merriment there were, in large measure, but few outbursts of wild hilarity or uncontrolled animal spirits.

Mrs. Kirby says that the Farm was a "grand place for children." They were quick to feel the sympathetic interest in their pleasure and work, and they too were affected by the general sense of freedom. One of the teachers in the infant school declined at first to accept this duty, on the ground that it was unwise to subject a young child to restraints for which he felt an instinctive and healthy dislike, such as sitting still and learning the primer. Mrs. Kirby and Miss Abby Morton both gave efficient service in this section of the school, which was reorganized under a stricter discipline when the Fourier movement took possession of the place.

Miss Marianne Ripley presided over the primary department, and had with her in the

Nest the two sons of George Bancroft, George
and John; the two Spanish boys from Manila,
Lucas and José Corrales; and James Lloyd
Fuller, the youngest brother of Margaret
Fuller. The latter had no intention of remaining a neglected genius, and it is recorded
of him that he kept a diary which it would
be absurd to call private, since it was his habit
to tear out pages and leave them about so
that the objects of his displeasure could not
well avoid finding them.

The curriculum of the preparatory school
had always included such branches as Latin,
Italian, German, moral philosophy, and the
English classics; but the advent of many young
men for the special purpose of study made it
necessary to introduce Greek, mathematics, and
other advanced courses. There were students
from Manila, Havana, Florida, and Cambridge
— for Harvard College indicated Brook Farm
as a fitting resort for young men whose conse-
cration to extra-collegiate interests rendered
them subjects for temporary seclusion, and
preferably a country life. Reasonably enough,
perhaps, botany was exceedingly popular with
those who were feeling their first real contact
with natural beauty; and since the neighborhood provided liberally in the way of specimens,
there was every excuse for rambles to wood and
river. Mr. Ripley taught mathematics and

philosophy, using Cousin as a text-book in his philosophy classes. Mrs. Ripley was responsible for imbuing many minds with a taste for history and modern languages. She had the power to transmit her own intensity of interest to most of those whom she instructed, and she inspired in them a genuine fervor for culture.

Dana's classes were in Greek and German, the latter being full of pupils who yearned not only to discover the beauties of German literature, but who admired the rather severe methods which the scholarly young tutor introduced. The shame of the youth who entered Dana's classroom with an unlearned lesson differed in quality from that which he felt in other class-rooms under the same circumstances. The teaching of music and Latin fell to the lot of John S. Dwight; in the former he was assisted by his sister Frances, and in the latter by his sister Marianne. So penetrating an influence was his musical instruction that there has been no occasion to consider his merit as a Latin teacher, although it seems just to believe that if he had done anything extraordinarily good or bad in this department, somebody would have noted it. A class in singing was started; the masses of Haydn and Mozart were gradually taken up; and in instrumental music the standard from the beginning was high. Music was not the only art which was encouraged. Miss Hannah

B. Ripley, a niece of George Ripley, taught drawing, and Miss Amelia Russell, who communicated life to the Association in many ways, gave lessons in dancing, which one suspects to have been much in demand. The department of belles-lettres was confided to George P. Bradford, a graduate of Harvard and a man of much cultivation and charm. His endeavors in behalf of unprofitable knowledge could not have been arduous among these "unworldlings."

At the end of the second year there were in the school thirty boys and girls, whose fathers and mothers believed with Mr. Fuller that it was a good thing to send children where they "would learn for the first time, perhaps, that all these matters of creed and morals are not quite so well settled as to make thinking nowadays a piece of supererogation, and would learn to distinguish between truth and the 'sense sublime,' and the dead dogma of the past." This was a rare demand on a secondary school, and rarer still was the disposition to meet it; but for this very reason the school could never have been popular. The wonder is not that this part of the institution declined under the later attacks of the press against Fourierism, but that it so long held its prestige. While it is manifestly impossible to gage the intellectual impetus referable to the Brook Farm school, it is equally impossible to ignore it in the face of much direct testimony and in view of the honorable career and high character of many of its students.

A son of Orestes A. Brownson was there; Miss Deborah Gannett, a niece of Ezra S. Gannett, familiarly known as Ora, who was notable for having dared to tease Hawthorne, and who afterward became the wife of Charles B. Sedgwick of Syracuse; Miss Caroline A. Kittredge, afterward married to James Theodore Allen of West Newton; Miss Sarah F. Stearns, a niece of Mrs. Ripley, who was also a member of the Association, and who became a Roman Catholic and entered a convent; Miss Annie M. Salisbury, who has published a little pamphlet on Brook Farm; Horace Sumner, a younger brother of Charles Sumner, — a delicate youth, of less intellectual force than his brothers and sisters, — whose admiration for Margaret Fuller led him to join her later in Europe, whither he had gone in quest of health, and who, returning with the Ossolis on the doomed *Elizabeth*, met his death with them, — these were all there at one time or another.

One young woman who was a pupil-teacher, and who should be especially considered, was Georgianna Bruce, afterward Mrs. Kirby, and quoted throughout this book under that name. She was about twenty-two years old when she went to Brook Farm on the agreement that she was to work eight hours a day for board and instruction. She had with her there a brother, fourteen years of age, who was also received as a pupil-worker. Her first duties were ironing on certain days, preparing vegetables for dinner every day, and helping to "wash up" after supper. At the end of a year she was admitted as a *bona fide* member of the Association, when it included only a dozen people. She was an English girl of reputable but somewhat humble birth. She early found that she had her own living to earn, and this she contrived to do in many and eventful ways. She had great vivacity, some sentimentality, and a disposition which might have been peppery had she not possessed sufficient discretion to control herself. After an experience in England and America, well calculated to develop her natural strength of character, she found herself in the family of Dr. Ezra Stiles Gannett, the Unitarian clergyman of Boston, as a sort of nursery governess. Imperfectly educated, she did not lack ambition, and was constantly seeking to improve herself. Her "Years of Experience" contain some lively chapters on Brook Farm, for she observed shrewdly, although she was not unappreciative, and she often does justice to her surroundings. In 1871 and 1872 she contributed several unsigned papers entitled "Reminiscences of Brook Farm" to *Old and New*. The narrative must not be taken too seriously, although it and her book have furnished a good share of the material usually drawn upon. She felt compelled to disguise real personages, and "in one or two instances to combine one character with another." This license and some palpable errors into which her imperfect recollection of things long past betrayed her, give almost the effect of a fictitious narrative. In view of the genuine kindness shown her and her somewhat troublesome brother, it has been intimated that her recollections betray signs of unfairness and an acid temper.

The Associates used to write many letters, not only to outsiders, but to each other, and at any time of day or night. The letter which follows was written certainly not before the summer of 1842, by Georgianna Bruce to a girl friend in Boston. It gives such a clear picture of the actual movement of the life at Brook Farm, and is so full of good spirits, that it is given entire. It is an admirable epitome of the earlier days.

EYRIE, BROOK FARM, *Saturday Night*.

I received yours, dearest, this afternoon by Dr. Dana, who, with I don't know how many others, was out here. We met Barbara Channing and others on the doorstep on our return from a boat ride. Three or four of the boys have clubbed together and bought a boat, painted it, fitted it up with sails, compass, etc., and especially a carpet (**Paris** they say) for the ladies' feet, in arranging which

they have taken, as you may suppose, clear comfort, as
well as kept clear of mischief of some sort, I dare say.
And this afternoon was the first time that it was honored
with our presence. Four of us girls, — Mary G.[annett],
Abby Morton, Caddy Stodder, and myself, with five boys,
— our Spanish Manuel being Captain *for the day*, — set
sail in Charles River after having walked a mile through
the fields and woods, not to mention swamps. We sailed
a good way up, passed under the Dedham bridge, then
down, singing away, Abby and I. Oh! the woods round
Cow Island are so rich, the young pale green birch, down
by the bank, contrasted with the dark tall pines, the sky
with just enough of *life* in the clouds to satisfy me, and
the deep water with just a ripple on the surface, and so
warm that you could hold your hand in, formed a picture
that seemed perfect. But then came in *man* to mar and
disfigure. Two men with hatchets cutting down those
same beautiful trees and another with a line hooking the
fish (for mere amusement, most likely). I really sympa-
thize with Mr. Bradford who writes me that "in cutting
down the green young branches for pea-sticks he is really
afraid of the vengeance of the wood demon and looks
around to see if any Brownies are near." Well, we got
home perfectly safe as I informed you, and after tea a
large party of all sorts came up here to hear some music,
so here I must stop to tell you that to my inexpressible
joy the piano and Mr. Dwight have at length come. The
piano is a handsome one of a sweet tone, and Mr. D. has
some of the best of music which I use, principally German. You will know that every spare moment is devoted
to music now. We are going to get up a glee club forth-
with. George and Burrill Curtis (of whom I will speak
or perhaps have spoken before) take the bass and tenor,
I and Abby the soprano and second. Then a large number who know very little about music are going to commence
with the rudiments. Poor Mr. D. said to-night, when we

were washing up the tea things with two or three of the
gentlemen wiping, and groups here and there discussing,
"How *fast* you *live* here; I *like* it, but really my head,
my head suffers," and then we had a talk about it, and
Burrill said that he had noticed how we seemed to drive
with everything, but that we were in debt and must not
therefore be at leisure, and that we must be willing to
bear the consequences of the errors and sins of past time
for a season, and after all he could not think of living in
the old way again; it seemed like stagnation, vegetation.
Burrill is not of age, and his brother only eighteen. They
both have large fortunes, I believe, and have come out
of the most fashionable society of New York, their father
entirely absorbed in *banks* and dollars. Burrill is a perfect beauty, entirely unconscious, and then (as Sarah
[Stearns] says) so human. If you speak to him, he listens
as if he thought there was *at least* a chance that you were
worth listening to. He stands alone and acts for himself.
His brother looks to him and is unconsciously influenced
by him. George has a rich voice and they sing duets
together — the Irish melodies which I love so much,
etc. George plays beautifully and entirely by ear. Is it
not grand to see them come out so independently and
work away at the peas!!! We have had the Mortons from
Plymouth to make a visit, leave two of their boys and
Abby, and choose a building spot. You would like Mr.
M. He looks just as you can fancy the most loving of
the Puritans looked, and really *is* one, divested of all their
superstition and bigotry. He read a letter to us before
he left, that he had written to a nephew now in Germany,
explaining the community principles, etc. I wish you
could have heard it. It is so strange, as well as pleasant,
to hear the ideas which different persons entertain of the
same subject, expressed in their own peculiar way; and
really if I should judge by the most beautiful letters I
have read, written by one and another among us, I should

think that our *grandchildren* would not waste time were they to collect some of them if they wanted to trace the history of the *first community*.

We number over sixty and several more are coming. We have now a long table in the entry. Mrs. Barlow is going to New York for a week, and I have offered to take the *joys* and cares of a mother to her two boys during her absence, concerning which duties and pleasures we have had no little merriment. "*Orah dear*" [Gannett] has not returned, but her sister Mary has come — a smart, pleasant, trusting child. Of course I do not love her as well as Orah yet, but I have a sort of a *motherly* feeling to her, and she turns to me as one does to a sister. To-morrow I must write her. Only think of my writing all this after twelve o'clock with Sarah snoring away, and Sophia [Ripley] would not hear of my practising. And now I have not told you of the beautiful wild flowers I found in the woods and gave them to Mr. Dwight because he loves them, nor of how I took my scholars to walk this morning and we sang in the woods. But I must say good night, dearest, or shall lose my breakfast to-morrow. Now you will kiss dear little Kit for me, won't you? and give my love to all. I had an invitation to ride in and out last Sunday, but having sprained my ankle and not feeling very well, I did not think that even to *see you* I ought to risk making myself more sick. I got the medicine, etc. Be sure and come out if you can; I have much to tell you which I cannot write. I took a walk in the woods to-night. If I am ever so tired or excited, this always has a calming, quieting influence.

Your loving sister,

GEORGY.

Postscript. What a horrid matter of fact concern this is; but you must take what there *is*, not what you wish for, and the spirit moved in the direction of *facts*. Do come and spend the day if you can with Mary Anne.

I have just thought of the interesting fact that if I had related the story of the boat in Boston to any one not feeling as much interested as yourself, without specifying the ages of the boys, 15–19, etc., it would have been reported round that at Brook Farm the little boys were allowed to go on the river at all times and seasons without any restraint, and that a *few* had already been drowned !

The terms for board and tuition, including all branches, is five dollars for a girl and four for a boy per week. This includes music, drawing, etc., there being no extra charges except washing.

Mrs. Kirby's fellow-teacher in the infant school, Abby Morton, has, as Mrs. Diaz, become known in American literature for the excellent quality of her humor. The author of the "William Henry" books is even more thoroughly imbued to-day with the spirit of Brook Farm than she was during her slight affiliation with the community.

Dr. John Thomas Codman, whose book, "Brook Farm : Historic and Personal Memoirs," is the most comprehensive account as yet published, is still living, and practising the profession of dentistry in Boston. Dr. Codman has told his own story so generously that little remains to say, beyond the important fact that, although he did not arrive as a pupil with his parents and brother and sister until March, 1843, when some of the choicest spirits were

G

already gone, and although he stayed on well into the bitter end, he champions the cause of his youth with undimmed ardor. He saw the worst, and is the most copious witness of the latter days and still he is a Brook Farmer. His brother Charles H. Codman was also there, and lived to carry his early imbibed principles into the conduct of his picture shop. This brother died by a painful accident on September 18, 1883. The sister Rebecca married Butterfield, one of the printers of the *Harbinger*, and is still living.

Two of the students afterward achieved reputation as able soldiers in the Civil War. One — General Francis Channing Barlow — was born on October 19, 1834, in Brooklyn, New York, and was graduated at Harvard College in the class of 1855. Though a lawyer by profession, at the opening of the Civil War he was doing editorial work on the *Tribune*. Entering the volunteer service as a private, he was soon commissioned as Lieutenant Colonel of the Sixty-first Regiment, New York Volunteers, and was made Brigadier General in September, 1862, for distinguished services at Fair Oaks. He was twice severely wounded, was with Grant in the late campaigns of the Army of the Potomac, and was mustered out with the rank of Major General. From the State of New York he held the office of Secretary of State, from 1865 to

1868, and of Attorney General, from 1871 to 1873, when he was instrumental in the prosecution of the Tweed Ring. During the last twenty years of his life he was a brilliant member of the New York bar, and died on January 11, 1896.

Another soldier, Colonel George Duncan Wells, was a youth of about fifteen, whose connection with the Farm has seldom been mentioned, although he prepared for college there under Dana's particular attention. He was a Greenfield boy and was a fine, manly fellow, with long blond curls; erect and handsome, he was equally attractive to the young and old of both sexes, and the young boys especially conceived a high admiration for his superior skill in all youthful sports. Arthur Sumner, a pupil who has published some interesting pages of recollections, refers with enthusiasm to his appearance as an Indian brave in the famous "gypsy picnic." He entered the Sophomore class at Williams in 1843, showing evidences of unusual training for his age. The activity and grasp of his mind, his superior literary taste, especially in poetry, and his wide reading occasioned general comment. After studying law in Greenfield and at Harvard, he practised it for several years in Greenfield; he served two terms in the Massachusetts Legislature, attracting more than

ordinary notice both as a lawyer and as a legis-
lator, on account of his brilliant forensic ability;
in 1859 he became a justice of the Police Court
in Boston.

When the war broke out, Wells, though far
from sympathizing with the abolition sentiment,
threw himself into the movement for the preser-
vation of the Union. Like General Butler, he
would have been glad if this consummation had
been possible without the necessity of freeing a
single slave, and he frankly stated his position
in his recruiting speeches. He was appointed
Lieutenant Colonel of the First Massachusetts
Infantry on May 22, 1861, and became Colonel
of the Thirty-fourth Massachusetts Infantry on
July 11, 1862. His efficiency as an officer may
be justly inferred from the requests entered at
different times, at the War Department, by
Hooker and Doubleday, to have the Thirty-
fourth Massachusetts sent to them as a special
favor. Such commendation indirectly confirms
the testimony of his official associates that he
was brave and cool, strict in discipline, and yet
never unmindful of the comfort of his men;
jealous of the reputation of his regiment, but
anxious to recognize good service on the part of
any of his soldiers. One reminiscence which
calls up the traditions of Brook Farm states
that "the Colonel and Chaplain have thus far
been masters of the butter which is, neverthe-

less, decidedly strong; but the rest confess themselves beaten."

Wells was mortally wounded on October 13, 1864, in a skirmish which preceded the battle of Cedar Creek, and the diary of his successor contains these words: "God only knows how tenderly and sincerely we all loved him. The 34th has lost its idol."

Among the young men at Brook Farm there was a high level of good looks, but no others excited so much attention as the two Curtis brothers. *Ambo Arcades* they certainly were, tall and strong of limb, graceful, and endowed besides with attractive social qualities. Burrill, as he was called, was two years older than his brother, who was born on February 24, 1824. Until the latter was twenty-five years of age the brothers were closely united, sharing all duties and pleasures. They were at school together at Jamaica Plain, at Providence, after their father's second marriage, at Brook Farm, and at Concord.

George William Curtis and James Burrill Curtis

Independence of opinion and freedom of conduct do not always coexist, but an entire self-assertiveness showed early in George Curtis. The experience at Brook Farm, with the constant though good-natured clash of theories, could not prove other than valuable to his unformed character, for he is properly to be considered as a scholar, not as a full associate. Able as the

brothers were through fortunate circumstances to
do what seemed desirable to them, they were by
no means free from the impressionability of
youth, and fell under the double spell of Emerson's genius and the vague but alluring influence
of Transcendentalism. It was natural, therefore, that they should, in 1842, go to Brook
Farm, where they became boarders for two
years, George being twenty years of age when
the stay ended. They were industrious in their
studies of German and of agricultural chemistry,
but in particular of music under Dwight. It is
probable that they took a hand in more exact-
ing pursuits, even when their spirit of gallantry
made no suggestions, for when Arthur Sumner
first saw George he was "chopping fagots with
a bill-hook behind the Eyrie all alone;" but for
picnics these "young Greek gods," as Miss
Russell calls them, had a genuine predilection.
It has often been told how the younger of the
two, dressed in a short green skirt, danced as
Fanny Elssler — a celebrity much in vogue in
those days. The same kindly memory recalls a
picture of George Curtis and George Bradford,
on cold, stormy washing days, "hanging out the
clothes for the women — a chivalry equal to
that of Walter Raleigh throwing down his cloak
before the Queen Elizabeth."

They were true amateurs throughout their
brief stay, and there is nothing to show that

they held more than a well-bred complaisance
toward the various phases of cultivated radicalism. George, in writing to his father, to whom
he seems never to have yielded a single point
of opinion, said, having the Farm in view: "No
wise man is long a reformer, for wisdom sees
plainly that growth is steady, sure, and neither
condemns nor rejects what is or has been.
Reform is organized distrust." In after life all
that he said of these two years was softened
by the gracious autumnal mist of memory; if
there was any sourness in his recollections, he
concealed it. It is possible to exaggerate, also
possible to underrate, the effect upon him of the
Brook Farm experience. A practical soul who
disliked Curtis's views on the rights of women,
once flung out his conviction that "there must
be a screw loose somewhere in a man who
graduated from that lunatic school at Brook
Farm." There was, however, a thread of
revolt in the pattern of his character, else Curtis would not have sought as he did almost
at once, in the company of his brother, the influence of Concord. Here, as at Brook Farm,
was the mixture of farm work and of association
with cultivated minds. The brothers simply
passed from one grade to another of the same
curriculum. Undue parental restriction would
have worked no wise result in the upbringing
of a young man who could ask his father:

"What does it matter to me or God whether Lowell or Manchester be ruined?" A believer in a high tariff might well have despaired, as David for Absalom, over a son who left a Rhode Island merchant as an interested third party out of such a calculation.

When the Curtises left Brook Farm, they must for a time have created a void. A love for all that is beautiful had its place among the residents there, and when George Ripley spoke of the "two wonderfully charming young men," it was with that same fondness with which Miss Russell mentions Burrill as having a typical Greek face and long hair falling to his shoulders in irregular curls. Of George she notices that, though only eighteen years old, he "seemed much older, like a man of twenty-five possibly, with a peculiar elegance, if I may express it — a certain remoteness of manner, however, that I think prevented persons from becoming acquainted with him as easily as with Burrill." In recording his contribution to the music at Brook Farm, Mrs. Kirby tells with gratitude that Curtis was never "guilty of singing a comic song."

In spite of the potent influence of Emerson, and later of the direct companionship at Concord, during intervals of farm work, of Emerson himself, and of Hawthorne, Thoreau, Alcott, and the poet Channing, "the extremely practical, unspeculative quality of his mind was making itself felt." Determined on a career of literature, he first put forth in 1845 a few letters from New York to the *Harbinger*. The brothers did not leave Concord, however, until they had fully tried the merits of a combination of physical labor and intellectual life. They delved, while they thought, in their three separate residences, first with Captain Nathan Barrett, who speedily set them to getting out manure to "test their metal," next with Edmund Hosmer, and last with Minot Pratt, — all of them capable of appreciating the young men beyond their mere capacity as amateur "hands" for farm work.

After the interesting and profitable sojourn at Concord, both Burrill and George returned to New York, and then travelled much in Europe, where they went in 1846, and where Burrill remained for four years. "Our cousin the Curate" in "Prue and I" gives, it is said, a sketch of Burrill, softened and modified from the actual personality. Burrill went finally to England, where he was a curate in Cambridge; he received the degree of Master of Arts from Cambridge University. He died about two years ago. Colonel Higginson says that Burrill was the more interesting and perhaps the handsomer. He was at one time during his stay at Brook Farm passing through a trying experience, and may on that account have excited a more than usual degree of interest and sympathy; but in leaving this country, he faded gradually from public memory.

After George Curtis's return from Europe he entered definitely into literature; his first important venture being the "Nile Notes of a Howadji" (1851). The book was clever and successful, but it called down on its author some censure, as did also the "Howadji in Syria," published a year later. After half a century the effect of these books is still fresh and strong. They are glowing with an Occidental's feelings toward the East, and have caught the true spirit of *impressions de voyage*, early instances in American literature of this delicate mode of expression in which the French have been so long masters. It is clear that George William Curtis came out of the East a pretty well sophisticated young man, and not unduly coy or incommunicative.

The two books show a man naturally sensitive and delicate, but impressionable to a vague and sensuous atmosphere. Mr. Chadwick says that the "Howadji" marked an "exquisite satirical recoil from the pretence of holiness in things and places which could claim no genuine associations with the Christian origins." It is, however, true that Curtis, even as early as the Brook Farm days, allowed himself certain expressions which show that in his early manhood there was an alloy. In his next book, "Potiphar Papers," Curtis undertook to scourge the evils of a society of which he was an ingratiating and willing member, and the *sæva indignatio* of the true satirist is therefore wanting. He who said that he could see no satire in "Vanity Fair" never went farther himself than to assail palpable vulgarity and the superficial aspects of fashionable life. In the "Potiphar Papers," he was clearly following Thackeray, but he missed the ethical soundness which lay beneath Thackeray's literary effects. Yet this book has its severities and its sincerities, and contains some excellent and memorable passages. It was Mrs. Potiphar who said: "In a country where there's no aristocracy one can't be too exclusive." If there was a touch of cynicism it came from a youth. As Curtis grew older, his thrusts were more graceful — not less vigorous. His "Belinda and the Vulgar," in the Easy Chair, proclaims his social creed, wherein appears a geniality which was earlier wanting in the cosmopolitan Kurz Pacha of the "Potiphar Papers," — a very terrible and cutting fellow until he is discovered to be only Curtis disguised in a costumer's garb as a far-travelled Oriental.

"Prue and I," which followed, was of so different a quality from the "Potiphar Papers" that it may have taken off the edge of relish for the not especially dangerous cynicism of the latter. Its idealism was unrestrained, placing as it did the solution of human happiness frankly

in the hands of the poor man, and almost deny-
ing to the rich his allotted cup of cold water. It
won a place in the hearts of men rather than in
their heads, for such a view of life is comforting.
The steady-headed Prue is Curtis's concession
to established facts, and in her character he
anticipates a later theory that men are the born
idealists, and women the practical element of
life, though at no period was he a partisan of
the merits of either sex.

At this time, and on occasions during the rest
of his life, Curtis gave lectures of the older type
as best represented by Emerson and Phillips.
He had a good share in maintaining the repute
of that civilizing institution, the lyceum, a valued
adjunct to American educative methods. In
1856 he made himself responsible for the payment of a large sum through the failure of *Putnam's Monthly*, and it was nearly twenty years
before this debt was discharged. Such a simple
act of duty strengthened the tissues of character
and transformed the glowing youth which conceived the Howadji books into a robust manhood
which never failed him. Life moved henceforth for Curtis with the swiftness of the events
in which he was to take an active part until his
death. He was already editor of *Harper's
Weekly*, then more powerful than any similar
publication can hope to be again. Impersonal and moderate in his editorial work, he

was nevertheless a favorable, not extravagant, instance of the " one-man power " in journalism, now so much and so regrettably lessened.

Not until the last third of his career did he evince his admirable powers of oratory, for which he had a special qualification — a voice so musical and gracious that the compass was not at first perceptible. Curtis's voice was memorable in the old Brook Farm days. Not of the most commanding order, which sways vast bodies of men and for the while convinces them, his eloquence may be compared not unfavorably with that of the late Robert C. Winthrop. Though lacking somewhat the ripest cultivation, it did not fall short of what constitutes a high degree of forceful and scholarly utterance.

The latter part of Curtis's life was best spent in promulgating the duty of parting company with whatsoever political party shall fail to satisfy the conscience of the voter, regardless of close affiliations. He also gave severe labor to the work of reforming the national civil service, and for this unselfish toil there is already assured to his name the gratitude of honest men. In both these efforts he was as successful as one may fairly be in a political system still flowing abundantly with milk, honey, and compromise. As he lacked the robustness needful for partisanship, so proportionally he lacked greatness, according to the measure of American political life, and therefore what he really did accomplish was the more remarkable. To the Easy Chair of *Harper's New Monthly Magazine*, he contributed about fifteen hundred essays, the charm of which is likely to be a treasured memory in our letters. They served many good causes, and among them the spread of a true cosmopolitanism. Did any good man or woman of more than local value die, he embalmed the fragrance of such a life in one of these delightful essays.

If it be true that he who is not with a movement is against it, then surely Curtis is not entitled to be thought a true product of Brook Farm. He had not the essential qualities of a reformer; there is no evidence that he was ever so wedded to a cause that he was ready to suffer for it. His blow was steady, his purpose honest, but there was lacking the terrible, implacable strength, which persists past any hazard, until the gates of sin are forced. He wanted the world to be better; but he would accomplish the result in a gracious — shall we say in a comfortable? — manner.

Before Father Hecker died, he had
Isaac Thomas Hecker travelled widely in spirit and in practice from Brook Farm. He never, however, showed ingratitude toward his immediate associates for whom he had baked, and with whom he had broken, bread. His progress of life,

from the early wrestlings against the dangers
of commerciality, throughout his brief sojourn-
ing in Brook Farm, Fruitlands, and Concord,
and during his steady advance toward the Catholic Church, was continuous and consistent. He
was born on December 18, 1819, of German immi-
grant parentage; from the mother, who had an
equable temperament and much good sense, he
probably received the better part of his intellectual inheritance. His two older brothers
and himself learned the baker's trade, and
eventually built up a prosperous business. He
is remembered to have said, in speaking of his
earlier years: "I have had the blood spurt out
of my arm carrying bread when I was a baker,"
and this untempered zeal for the task at hand
followed him into the priesthood. Although he
studied hard and constantly, Hecker could not
fairly be called an educated man or a thoroughly trained priest. One must have no little
sympathy with such a life as Hecker's to judge
it with fairness or toleration. Wholesome and
open-hearted from his youthful days, when he
felt a strong aversion to being touched by
any one, he had an element of unusualness,
which soon developed mystical tendencies, and
finally a complete reliance on the workings of
supernatural forces within him.

Long before his twentieth year Hecker had
plunged violently into active political life under

the influence of Brownson, who, in the early
thirties, was devoting his tremendous energies
to bringing the Workingmen's Party to recognition in New York. When Hecker was less
than fifteen years of age he carried through
some important resolutions at the ward meetings of his party. He and his brothers once
invited the menace of law by printing across the
back of bills received from customers a quota-
tion, attributed to Daniel Webster, proclaiming
the virtues of a paper currency. This political
fervor came to nothing definite beyond teaching
the lad self-reliance and knowledge of men, but
it was the means of confirming a friendship
with Brownson, "the strongest, most purely
human influence, if we except his mother's,
which Isaac Hecker ever knew," to use the
words of his competent biographer, Father
Elliott. The critical period of youth he passed
with singular purity and simplicity of conduct,
and a display of stoical tendencies which developed into asceticism. His falling in with Brownson marked also the beginning of a distinctly
religious phase, and henceforth each of these
two men, in his own way, travelled the same
road toward the same goal, Hecker arriving
there a little before his older friend.

Eight years after meeting so fateful an acquaintance he found himself at Brook Farm,
but the intervening years brought him many

peculiar spiritual experiences, or "visitations," as it seems proper to call them. He kept inwardly debating the necessity of parting with his brothers so far as regarded his business career, but at no time does he appear to have refused their generous aid. His own solitary path was certainly made easier by their willingness to maintain him in it. Brownson, sympathizing with his spiritual distress, advised a residence at Brook Farm, and wrote to Ripley with this plan in view. Hecker went there in January, 1843, and on March 6 wrote to his brother George: "What was the reason of my going, or what made me go? The reason I am not able to tell. But what I felt was a dark, irresistible influence upon me that led me away from home. . . . What keeps me here I cannot tell." A little later he urged his brother not to "get too engrossed with outward business." What would have been the solution of Isaac Hecker's difficulties had his brothers forsaken an honorable calling at the bidding of an inward voice? He entered Brook Farm as a "partial" boarder at four dollars a week, and gave his services as a baker in exchange for instruction, at first in German philosophy, French, and music. Curtis, whose kindly but reserved memories of him are almost the only recollections of this period, speaks of him as not "especially studious"; but he found him a young man of "gentle and

H

affectionate manner," with "an air of singular
refinement and self-reliance, combined with a
half-eager inquisitiveness"; and it was Curtis
who disclosed to Hecker that the latter was undoubtedly the original of Ernest the Seeker in
W. H. Channing's story of that name which appeared in the *Dial*. Hecker did not long continue to bake for the common good, for while the
honest bread rose, his spiritual thermometer was
falling. He soon became a "full" boarder, pay-
ing for the greater freedom five dollars and a half
a week, furnished, we may suppose, by his hard-
working brothers. Details of Hecker's life at
the Farm are wanting, but that he was looked
upon as eccentric and shy is evident from the
rather faint impression left. The start was in-
auspicious, according to Mrs. Kirby, who says:
"I learned the next day that the new comer,
who was a baker by profession and a mystic by
inclination, had been nearly crazed by the
direct rays of the moon, which made the circuit
of the three exposed windows of his room."

Father Elliott sees in the associative experiment a working toward a high ideal, realizable
only in the supernatural order of his church.
So far as association was a revolt, in the natural
or unconverted life, against selfishness and unrestrained individualism, it was commendable.
"These West Roxbury adventurers were worthy
of their task, though not equal to it." He does

not find among them "the slightest evidence of
sensuality, the least trace of the selfishness of
the world, or even any sign of the extravagances
of spiritual pride," but contrasts Frédéric Oza-
nam's success with the failures of George Ripley and of Saint Simon, whom he pronounced
to be a "far less worthy man." Both Hecker
and Brownson found the generally tolerant spirit
of the place refreshing. Their association with
men and women of noble aspirations was helpful, and neither of them failed in a reasonable
gratitude toward this early experience. Both
of them, in later years, bore frank testimony to
the more trying features of the Church which
they followed; and the entire want of vulgarity
and low ambitions at Brook Farm may often
have been silently, perhaps regretfully, remembered. Strongly under the spell of Brownson's
forcible manner, Hecker did not wholly confine
himself to discipleship, but went over to West
Roxbury to hear Parker, to Concord to see
Emerson, and no doubt to Boston, where everything strange and improbable was then herded
together as in an ark.

Outwardly he appears to have made a favorable impression by reason of his candor and
amiability; but there is evidence that inwardly
all was not well with him. His journals show
that he alternately drew toward the Church, and
then in cold doubt fell shrinkingly back. It

was strange as it was tragic that toward the close of his life, after long years in the priesthood, he again fell into dark moods. Up to the time of his leaving Brook Farm he had settled the one point that he would never "join a Protestant church."

Supernatural experiences were not the only ones which troubled Hecker's serenity at Brook Farm. There is reason to think that he felt the influence of what, in the commonplaces of religion, is called an "earthly love," and that he might even have wooed and married like other men; but in season to prevent this conclusion there came strongly upon him the vision of a mystical espousal and union which rendered him "no longer free to invite any woman to marriage." Notwithstanding his convictions in this matter, Hecker was advised frankly not to trust to supernaturalism in the matter of the affections.

On July 5, 1843, he writes: "To leave this place is to me a great sacrifice. I have been much refined by being here." On the eleventh of the same month he went to Fruitlands in search of "a deeper life"; and if getting one's eyes opened to harsh realities in less than two weeks is deepness of any kind, he certainly found what he sought. On July 12 he raked hay, and joined in a conversation on "Clothing"; the next day a conversation was held on "The

Highest Aim." But on July 21 Mr. Alcott asked him for his "first impressions as regards the hindrances . . . noted since coming here." Hecker thereupon gave him his objections in five heads, the chief of which were Alcott's want of frankness, and the fact that the place had very little fruit on it. A deficit of frankness and of fruit was not in the alluring programme offered to Hecker by Alcott earlier in the year; but to attempt to square Mr. Alcott's programmes with his achievements is like wrestling with a ghost. On July 25 Hecker left Fruitlands for Brook Farm on his way to New York. Hecker's biographer not unjustly says that "Fruitlands was the caricature of Brook Farm"; Hecker himself more mildly asserts that "Fruitlands was very different from Brook Farm, — far more ascetic," — as places are apt to be in which there is naught to digest but platitudinous conversations. He was not, however, so sparing of Alcott, who, he said, "was his own God." Alcott on his part went to Charles Lane and said: "Well, Hecker has flunked out. He hadn't the courage to persevere. He's a coward." Mr. Alcott was not always Orphic in his sayings.

For a while Hecker tested according to his ability various forms of philosophy and of religious beliefs, becoming once much interested, though hardly more than that, in Anglicanism.

On the very moment of crossing the threshold
of Catholicism he found himself at Concord, in
April, 1844, where he lodged at the house of
Henry Thoreau's mother. He had already refused to consider the offer of a room, furnished,
and with "good people," for seventy-five dollars
a year; and he now arranged with this excellent
lady for a room, "a good straw bed, a large
table, a carpet, washstand, bookcase, stove,
chairs, looking-glass," and lights for seventy-
five cents a week. Never, surely, was the inward light maintained at less cost to the lodger
and at less profit to the landlady.

In June, 1844, he went to Boston to confer
with Bishops Fenwick and Fitzpatrick; the latter questioned him regarding Brook Farm and
Fruitlands, seeming desirous to learn more of
his supposed socialist theories, and finally gave
him a letter to Bishop McCloskey, who on
August 1, 1844, gave him baptism; on the next
day Hecker made confession.

Before Hecker went to Belgium in 1845, he
proposed to Thoreau that they should go to Rome
together, but the latter stated that he had now "re-
tired from all external activity in disgust, and his
life was more Brahminical, Artesian-well, Inner-
Temple like"; this was Thoreau's way of escaping the fervor of a young convert. In September
of the same year, Hecker began his life in the
Redemptorist Novitiate of St. Trond in Belgium.

He found the discipline severe under the novice master, Father Othmann, but he added self-inflicted severities of his own. Acting under "impulses of grace," he tried to conquer the tendency to sleep. In October, 1846, he took the vows of obedience, poverty, and chastity. He then went at once to Wittem, where, for two years, he was to study philosophy and Latin. At the end of this time Brother Walworth, his companion, was ordained priest, but Isaac Hecker, having failed to satisfy his superior, remained simply a brother. The causes of this failure to advance are so evident, and the results from this time to the end of life were so disastrous, that it is highly important to speak without reserve. After he had left Brook Farm and had returned to New York, there is an entry in his diary for August 30, 1843, as follows: "If the past nine months or more are any evidence, I find that I can live on very simple diet,—grains, fruit, and nuts. I have just commenced to eat the latter; I drink pure water. So far I have had wheat ground and made into unleavened bread, but as soon as we get in a new lot, I shall try it in the grain." Two years before his death Hecker, who was not without an excellent sense of humor, speaking of these experiments, said: "Thank God! He led me into the Catholic Church. If it hadn't been for that I should have been one of the worst cranks in the world." There are several other entries as to his dietetic abuses. In November, 1844, he despairingly cries, "I wish I could dispense with the whole digestive apparatus!" At Concord he makes mention of *ein herrliches Essen* of "bread, maple sugar, and apples." He proposed for the Lenten season of 1845 to confine himself to one meal a day. It is not surprising then, after this outrageous treatment of his physical nature, and after the moral and mental severities of his novitiate, that he should have been unequal to meet the requirements at Wittem. He became so stultified that he could not fix attention on his books, and lapsed into a condition of animal stupidity. Father Othmann advised him at St. Trond to become "*un saint fou*." Unable to study, he did humble services — carried fuel and baked bread — as at Brook Farm. There being no manner of doubt as to his holiness, whatever the opinion as to his sanity, he was allowed to go with Father Walworth to the Redemptorists at Clapham, England, and at last was ordained by Bishop Wiseman, in October, 1849. Shortly after, Hecker, with other priests, began their Redemptorist mission in America, having for their chief object the conversion of non-Catholics, — the one great purpose of Father Hecker till his death. Notwithstanding his temporary obfuscation of mind, in a few years Hecker was able to put forth his ablest and probably best-known book, "Ques-

tions of the Soul," and this was soon followed by
"Aspirations of Nature," which, as his biographer says, was "not so hot and eager in
spirit." His only remaining work of importance
was that which appeared as occasional contributions to the *Catholic World*, some years later;
these were in part gathered in book form, as
"The Church and the Age."

In 1857 a misunderstanding arose between
the American Redemptorists and their Head;
and on August 29 of that year Hecker was
expelled, on the ground that his going to Rome
in the cause of the American fathers was in
violation of his vows. After a long and painful
experience in Rome, where he strove coura-
geously for his convictions, Hecker, who had
won the mind and also the heart of his Holiness,
Pius IX., gained a signal triumph, not personal,
but in the interests of American Catholicism.
On March 6, 1858, by a decree of the Congregation of Bishops and Regulars, and by
the sanction of the Pope, all the American
fathers were dispensed from their vows. The
result was the speedy formation of the Paulist
Community, or, more correctly, the Missionary
Priests of St. Paul, the Apostle.

Under Hecker's leadership the Paulists flourished, and, aside from their zeal in bringing conversion to non-Catholics, soon made themselves
a menace to various forms of public evil, par-

ticularly to intemperance. Cleanliness and good
order, as well as godliness, had a part in Hecker's
methods; and he showed a willingness, not only
for supervision, but also for personal coöperation in the needful drudgery of the mission.
The inertness, not to say the indolence, of his
younger days gave place to a practical manhood.
His lectures were popular in the widest sense,
and he was a peer of the great lecturers of the
day. It is due to say that he touched the hearts
of Americans as a whole more closely than he
did those of his own faith. The narrowness
shown toward Catholics at that time was met
with an equal narrowness, and it is no wonder
that Hecker's largeness of manner was not
always understood or appreciated.

Hecker's prevision and insight brought the
powerful aid of ephemeral and periodical literature to the support of his Church. His Catholicism refused no agencies by which success was
to be won. He started the *Catholic World* in
1865, and in 1870 the *Young Catholic*, — both to-
day of a reputable order of religious magazines.
His Apostolate of the Press was largely pro-
moted by means of the Catholic Publication
Society.

In the midst of this busy life Father Hecker
was called on to pay the penalty of his early
experiments in that dangerous laboratory, his
physical nature. In 1871 his health began to

fail definitely; he kept for some time longer his mental strength, but his digestion and nerves were seriously impaired. He went abroad for health, but did not find it. Strange to say, he had a dread of death which followed him many years, but he made a peaceful end, which came on December 22, 1888. Three years before this he underwent strange depressions, during which he neglected the offices of his faith. This period seems to have been a revival of the unhappy experiences at St. Trond and Wittem.

It has been said, even sneeringly, that Father Hecker was a member of the "Yankee Catholic Church." If this allegation could fairly be brought against the son of German immigrants living in cosmopolitan New York, it would admirably summarize his best reputation. His love of freedom of the soul, and a large-mindedness which he had found and appreciated in others at Brook Farm, never deserted him. He was, in his day, the best interpreter of his church to the cool-minded, practical, American character. If those who heard him, and who read his books and sermons, did not fully understand or accept his religion, they did at least comprehend and accept him, and he was thus a useful intermediary between his unchanging faith and our swift, restless civilization.

Though Hecker's writings lack the extreme arrogance shown by Brownson, they have the advantage of continuity. Hecker did not bear mental fruitage until his great, and, as it proved, final choice; from that time his spoken and written thoughts expressed the results of experience and the accretions of belief, while Brownson's spiritual vicissitudes make him one of the least convincing of theological investigators. Years back the older man had accused the younger of a "tendency to mysticism, to sentimental luxury, which is really enfeebling your soul." This condition, doubtless real, was happily overcome, but the residuum of Hecker's intellectual possessions was not large. His faith absorbed so much of himself that there was too little potency left, especially in view of the fact that he addressed himself to non-Catholics. His last book, "The Church and the Age," does not lift the proclamation of dogma an inch above the level maintained by most controversialists, and in no way does it redeem the promise of "Questions of the Soul." Indeed, he failed, on the whole, to compass in literature results vouchsafed to him in his immediate field. Remembering that Hecker was never a scholar, and that he failed even as a student, it would be fairer to his reputation, both as a zealous and faithful priest, and as a man who exerted some influence on American thought and conduct, to pass by his somewhat thin and uninspiring pages and fall back on the tribute paid him by the

Abbé Xavier Dufresne of Geneva, who said: "In my opinion Father Hecker was, after Père Lacordaire, the most remarkable sacred orator of the century."

Father Hecker's efforts to bring his church into a closer understanding of the American spirit has of late given rise to a controversy which threatens to be bitter. To those who are outside the pale of ecclesiastical matters, these feuds have no real value or interest, but the attacks on "Américanisme" betray an anxiety too real to be concealed. Conservative opposition to the policy dear to the ablest and most influential prelates of the Catholic Church in America has become acrimonious. Even the memory of Hecker himself is not spared in Maignen's "Was Father Hecker a Saint?" The good Paulist has been quiet in his grave for more than ten years, but though dead he is yet speaking for a cause which must inevitably go forward. The distance from West Roxbury to Rome is not so long as it was when the young mystic walked the groves and meadows of Brook Farm.

CHAPTER IV

THE MEMBERS

EVEN Emerson admitted that Brook Farm was a pleasant place, where lasting friendships were formed, and the "art of letter writing" was stimulated. But he held, moreover, that impulse without centripetal balance was the rule among the members, who suffered from the want of a head, and experienced an "intellectual sansculottism." The members could not well quarrel with these pleasantries, nor with his calling their cherished dream "an Age of Reason in a patty-pan." Such strictures are phrases after all, even in an Emerson. But he went further when he made the charge that those whose resolves were high, did not work the hardest, and that the stress fell on the few. This, however, is but one of the "necessary ways" of life which Emerson himself upheld.

Charles Lane, in an article contributed to the *Dial* (vol. iv.) and valuable as a contemporary opinion, was more searching. He found at Brook Farm an entire absence of assumption and pretence, but thought that taste, rather

than piety, was the aspect presented to the eye.
" If the majority in numbers," he continues,
" were considered, it is possible that a vote in
favor of self-sacrifice for the common good would
not be very strongly carried." There being no
profession of hand-to-hand altruism, — the word
was not then in the vernacular, — no charge of
hypocrisy can be lodged. Lane also thought
that riches would have been as fatal as poverty
to the true progress of the Association, and
herein he confirmed what had already been proclaimed. Endowments were early recognized
as possible agents for weakening the purposes
and activities of the experiment. If, as Mrs.
Kirby says, Brook Farm was a protest against
the *sauve qui peut* principle, then the stringen-
cies and little economies were no bad discipline,
and the display of a full purse would have been
an offence against the ethics of the place.
There was no mean poverty as there was no
parade of individual wealth.

It would be an injustice to the good sense
which underlay the external artificiality of this
life, to say that the people who assured to the
Association a lasting memory cherished any
special faith in the immediate success of the
undertaking. Twenty-five years had been set as
a reasonable limit for the accomplishment of the
high purposes announced. It is probable that
Ripley and Dwight were the really sanguine

ones ; for the influential members, as a body, must be fairly credited with a modicum of that ordinary human judgment which recognizes the adventitious quality of any new enterprise. These hoped for good fortune ; but they were prepared for partial failure at least.   When the community dissolved, the majority of its members met the crisis with a good-natured stoicism common to Americans.   The hopes of the over-buoyant could not fall far, for the issues of success or failure had not rested on their shoulders ; and those who had grumbled could easily find another opportunity.   Brook Farm, like college life, was a slow-working inspiration to those of ordinary endowment who, in after years, prospered moderately through their contact with free and wholesome influences in the Association. One member of the later group, William H. Teel, writing twenty-five years after, made the acknowledgment that what little he possessed of "education, refinement, or culture and taste for matters above things material," he owed to this alma mater "by adoption."   He probably voiced a gratitude felt by other inconspicuous members in their maturer years.

Had everybody who wished to join the Association been allowed to do so, the result had been strange indeed.   Political exiles, tradesmen in a small way who had failed elsewhere, ministers without parishes but generally with good-sized families, and needy widows, were among the applicants. Sometimes a whole family would present itself unannounced, and be sent away for want of room, if for no other reason. Inconsequent people, once admitted, were naturally the first to grumble at the Board of Direction over necessary retrenchments, though ready to sound the praises of the associative principle when affairs went to their liking.

One great step in genuine reform was taken noiselessly, and therefore with greater certitude, by both the antislavery and the transcendental movements. Men and women stood on a basis, not of asserted equality, but of actual achievement and assumed responsibility. Such publications as the *Liberty Bell* and the *Dial*, to name no others, show what a parity of sentiment and intellectual force there really was. This desirable condition had certainly never before shown itself publicly in American life. In the Brook Farm community, as in other phases of the radical tendencies of those days, there was a considerable number of women really capable of fellowshipping with men in a serious endeavor lying well outside of domestic relations. Even as late as 1844 there were but few married couples on the Farm. The maternal instinct, which is necessarily conservative, seemed to revolt against the project, while to masculine feelings it contained nothing inherently offensive.

I

Yet to blend domestic and associative sentiments was a part of the original plan. "Is it
not quite certain," dubiously asks Lane in the
Dial for January, 1844, "that the human heart
cannot be set in two places, that man cannot worship at two altars?" Emerson was more rudi-
mentary when he argued on behalf of mothers
that "the hen on her own account much preferred
the old way. A hen without her chickens was
but half a hen." The Brook Farm experiment
was mainly tested only by women of exceptional
courage — perhaps as the "happy-helpless an-
archists," which Emerson declared the Farmers
as a whole to have been; and this will explain
what Mrs. Kirby meant when she wrote that
there was no large mother nature at Brook
Farm; that, after the first period, the women
who came were inferior to the men; and that
the motive which influenced these new-comers
was livelihood rather than social melioration.
The earlier women threw away prerogative,
and gained the then doubtful privilege of
equality. The wonder is that those who first
went to Brook Farm did not invite a larger
share of censure from their own sex, but the
phenomenal innocence of the life there and the
absence of scandal, or of the least cause for it,
had much to do with a tolerance which lasted
until baseless attacks from a part of the New
York press caused a temporary odium. This

shadow did not fall, however, on Brook Farm
until its golden age was already gone and the
iron age of Fourierism fully begun.

There was religion at Brook Farm, but it was
by no means a religious community. Spiritual
culture, except in the case of particular individuals, was pursued more as a diversion or a
respite from more engrossing interests. Unitarianism might safely have included the majority
of the earlier members — it certainly was traditional with most of them. W. H. Channing's
visits never passed without services of deep interest and importance to a representative number
of the Associates. What there was of religious
life felt his stimulus. Although there was no
dogmatism, and "controversial discussion was
unknown," there is no recorded evidence of any
open, bold opposition to the accepted forms of
faith; there was, assuredly, no crudeness or
blatancy in this matter.

It has been said that toward the close some
definite interest was taken in Swedenborg's writings, but how much does not appear. A few —
a very few — passed from one or another form
of Protestantism to the Roman Catholic Church.
There is no pretence that this transition ever
threatened to assume the importance of a stam-
pede Romeward; nor would it be safe to assert
that discouragement at the failure of Brook
Farm affected those who sought this sheltering

fastness. The external charms of the historic faith have their fascinations even for those who never embrace it — and it is probable that some effect was produced by the strong arguments of Brownson. Hecker, formerly of their own flock, had gone with Brownson, and Charles Newcomb mysteriously flirted with the romanticism of the Church. This sort of fervor was in the air, and a few naturally followed their desires and tastes. It would be unnecessary even to mention this change of religious base in Mrs. Ripley and her niece, Miss Stearns, and in one or two more, were it not that too much stress has been given to the simple fact. There may possibly have been a touch of mysticism in the Brook Farm life; but Mrs. Kirby, for one, has exaggerated the actual condition when she says that "rough, wooden crosses and pictures of the Madonna began to appear, and I suspected rosaries rattling under the aprons." She is entirely in error when she says that Horace Sumner and Miss Dana became Catholics; the Miss Dana to whom she referred was not even in the Association. As for the Swedenborgian tendency there is this to say: Just as Catholicism represented the pendulum swung to its furthest point from rationalism, so did Swedenborgianism offer the extreme reaction from idealism, for in itself it is materialism — a holding out of merely creature comforts.

Death touched Brook Farm lightly,—a noteworthy fact, since there was a narrow escape from a fatal epidemic of smallpox, and no end of tampering with irregular theories of therapeutics. But the gravelly soil and the isolation from any centre of disease kept nearly every one in remarkably good health, and laid strong foundations for later years, when life became something more than a delightful experiment. The community did, however, suffer one loss in its six years of existence, in the death of Mary Ann Williams, who was buried with affectionate care in a portion of the Farm set apart for the Association's dead. One member of the later period, the Rev. John Allen, brought the body of his wife reverently to Brook Farm, where she was buried. These two graves were the only ones required during the whole period.

If death dealt gently with Brook Farmers, love made more havoc, though it is astonishing how little mismating there was. Intellectual equality and unusual opportunity for discovering real character would go far to explain the gratifying result. Fourteen marriages have been traced to friendships begun at Brook Farm, and the record of unhappy unions is small. There was one wedding at the Farm, that of John Orvis to John Dwight's sister, Marianne. At this simple ceremony W. H. Channing was the minister, and John Dwight made a speech of exactly five words. It is to be hoped that the earnest Channing pronounced them man and wife, and not "couply consociated"—a phrase which he suffered to be used in the *Present!*

Starting with about fifteen persons, the numbers never increased to above one hundred and twenty. By the time that the change to the Phalanx had been effected, nearly all the first comers were gone. A safe estimate would be that about two hundred individuals were connected with Brook Farm from first to last. Such names as were of especial lustre stand apart, as they would have stood in any condition, from their associates. Others, of a second rank, but of considerable importance, rise in memory whenever the name of Brook Farm is mentioned. By reason of individual vivacity, eccentricity, or earnestness of character, each helped to make this spot rich in associations. Nor have these personalities been wholly forgotten in the issue of their later years. But for their lives and their endeavors, Brook Farm would be less memorable, and it is therefore proper not to omit them from this record, intended primarily for the more notable among the members and visitors.

If it were possible, it would be interesting to trace the subsequent career of certain relatively unimportant members. One would like to know more for instance of Grandpa Treadwell, who was a merry soul, though a quiet one; or of Charles Hosmer, who had "the cranial development of a Webster." Christopher List, called "Chrysalis," who vied with Lizzie Curson in caring for visitors; Eaton, known as "Old Solidarity"; Colson, the shoemaker, with his wife; John and Mary Sawyer; Charles and Stella Salisbury, are some of the names which come and go without special relation to their consociates. The Misses Foord, of contrasting types of beauty, Dolly Hosmer, Mary Donnelly, pretty as her name half implies, — these and others of the women and girls, it is also difficult to trace beyond the fact that they once lived at the Farm. The undiscovered nicknames are tantalizing, for they are sometimes so full of unfulfilled promise. Who was Torquemada or Savonarola? Possibly Hecker and Parker. Who were Camilla and Sybilla, if not Cornelia Hall and Caroline Sturgis; and who, more than all, was Hawthorne's Dismal View, who soon abandoned the cheerful life as unsuited to his gloomy tastes?

Of several members, some of them humble in reputation and condition, but faithfully representative of the variegated membership, some brief notice deserves to be given.

Lewis K. Ryckman, a cordwainer, belonged to the "Shoemaking series" under the new order. His wife, short, sprightly, and nervous, played the part of hostess and attended to the women visitors. Ryckman was a thorough believer in the associate life, with its boundless promise to reduce the waste and purposeless friction of individual households, but he was no advocate of the sequestration of property,— "dried labor," as he called it; to him the impulse and ability to acquire was wholesome and proper, and he sought economy of social arrangement, not restriction of the individual. Ryckman went under the name of the Omniarch.

Ichabod Morton was a trustee from December, 1842, until April, 1843; his place on the Board was then taken by Minot Pratt. He was from Plymouth, and was the father of Mrs. Abby Morton Diaz. Emerson says of him that he was "a plain man and formerly engaged in the fisheries with success." Because he felt that sentiment rather than good business judgment governed the practical affairs of the Farm, he abandoned his purpose of joining the Association.

One of Hecker's successors at the honest task of baking was Peter M. Baldwin, known to all as the "General"—a tall, spare, osseous sort of man, built on the large Western plan, and thought to resemble Andrew Jackson. In spite of what has been written about an absence of tobacco smoke, it is certain that Baldwin loved this solacement as well as he did an argument. This saint in a green baize jacket and slippers, awkward and homely to view, was an idealist such as even Brook Farm marvelled at. He did not write it out like Hawthorne, or dream it as at Patmos, like Channing, but he baked it, uncomplainingly, and with a patience of the Abraham Lincoln type. Suddenly he departed out again into a world not so regardful as Brook Farm of unsuccessful fidelity. He was the first to leave after the fire, and really started the exodus which soon began in earnest. His adventurousness did not die with his departure. A little later he went to find gold in California, and died on the Pacific coast.

Another sturdy character, Thomas Blake, was given the title of "Admiral" in honor of his name, and because of a figure, gait, and make-up, which included a nautical hat and rolling collar. He was fond of life, and never shirked his share of work. Ephraim Capen was the "Parson," fond of reading in bed, and prone to fall asleep in the act. He was educated for the ministry, but lacked sufficient orthodoxy to preach dutifully the doctrine of eternal punishment. Frederick S. Cabot, the Corporation Clerk, was employed in the book-keeping department, and therefore deserving of his title of "Timekeeper." It is recorded that he enjoyed "dancing and fun."

Cabot was interested in the antislavery movement, and appears as an auditor of the accounts
of the Massachusetts Antislavery Society. His
going to Brook Farm seems to have occasioned
some criticism from his old friends; but in an
unpublished letter to Miss Caroline Weston,
dated December 1, 1844, from Brook Farm, he
defends his conduct on the ground that while
he loves the slave no less he loves humanity
more, and adds: " I feel that Association is
doing and will do more for Antislavery than
anything else can."

Arriving on the same day with Blake, John
Glover Drew, usually known as Glover, brought
with him the wholesome atmosphere of business
promptness and accuracy. Even his personal
appearance bespoke commercial ways and a
trig, well-groomed man. His advance was rapid
to the position of Commercial Agent and member of the Industrial Council, and he showed
himself a worthy shipper and forwarder of the
Farm's products and merchandise. Yet this
honest, determined comrade, so unlike many of
his associates, shared their faith, and helped to
improve their practice. Poetry was in his nature, but hidden under the smooth, careful raiment of a seeming prosperity. Associated with
Drew in the general expressing, shipping, and
purveying of the Farm was Buckley Hastings.
As a private enterprise the work which they

zealously performed might have been made profitable.

Another instance of a continued interest in social and industrial problems, originating in a brief residence at Brook Farm, is J. Homer Doucet (pronounced Douçay), an eclectic physician who is still practising in Philadelphia. He was born at Three Rivers, in Connecticut, in 1822, and was at the Association from the spring of 1844 to the summer of 1846, coming early enough to experience some of the first charm, and staying long enough to know the sadness of decay. Several papers of his reminiscences appeared during 1895 in the *Conservator*, a journal devoted to the memory of Walt Whitman and the cause of ethical culture. These recollections, from their evident sincerity and openness, have considerable value, and preserve several anecdotes which otherwise might have perished. A cordial tribute is paid by him to the excellence of the school, and to the refining and wholesome influences of the farm life. "I never heard," he writes, "loud or boisterous language used; I never heard an oath; I never saw or heard of any one quarrelling; I never knew that any one was ever accused or suspected of having acted in an ungentlemanly or unladylike manner anywhere on the place." His opinion of the potency of the land was low, yet he says that "we planted potatoes and raised very good crops." The strawberry bed, to which, according to him, the young ladies attended, stood near the Hive and did not make a good yield. Doucet lived in the Pilgrim House, but entered only two of its rooms, the ironing-room and his own, used during the day by the Sewing Group. The obvious nick-name of "Homer the Sweet" was bestowed on him.

Hospitality at Brook Farm was generous, but on one occasion it had fatal results. An Irish baronet, Sir John Caldwell, fifth of that title and Treasurer-General of Canada, appeared one day, bringing with him as valet an Irish-man named John Cheever. The baronet supped with the community on its greatest delicacy, pork and beans, and returned to the Tremont House, in Boston, where he died suddenly of apoplexy on the following day, October 22, 1842. Cheever had some little education, and the marks of a refinement beyond his station in life. He was commonly supposed to be the natural son of the baronet whom he served in so lowly a capacity. At all events, the forlorn-ness of Cheever's position, and the romantic circumstances of his birth moved Mr. Ripley and others to shelter him, not as a member, but as a sort of irregular attaché. The eccentrici-ties of his character added no little to the life of the community; his Irish wit and brogue were wholesome leaven, and he was on the whole a beloved inmate, though his tongue was voluble and sometimes sharp. Dr. Codman gives some instances of his oddities of dress and speech. He addressed Miss Ripley as "your Perpendicular Majesty," and during the later period would refer to the earlier members of the Association as "extinct volcanoes of transcendental nonsense and humbuggery." After Cheever left Brook Farm he went to the North American Phalanx; it is supposed that he fell into intemperate habits, which finally led to his mysterious disappearance.

"Sam" Larned is hardly more than a name in the annals of Brook Farm, and it is not known whether he was an associate, a scholar, or a boarder. Although he could not have been more than eighteen when he was there, he was given to all manner of ultraisms, and some delightful anecdotes centre about him. Robert Carter gives a vivid sketch of him in an article on "The Newness," published in the *Century* for November, 1889. Larned steadfastly refused at that time to drink milk on the ground that his relation to the cow did not justify him in drawing on her reserves; and when it was pointed out to him that he ought, on the same principle, to abandon shoes, he is said to have made a serious attempt to discover some more moral type of footwear. He later found radicalism somewhat wearisome, and became a Unitarian minister in Mobile, where he had married a slave-holding wife. He died in New York, of consumption, at the early age of twenty-eight.

Jean M. Pallisse was the Swiss engineer, an intelligent, placid man, fond of music to the point of playing dance tunes on his violin for the general festivities. He afterward went to New York, and filled a position of trust in a business house. Pallisse smoked tobacco, and was, therefore, a rare bird in this flock. Peter N. Kleinstrup, the Danish gardener, came early in the Fourier period with his wife and daughter. The greenhouse was built for him, but he did not, as has been stated, make his home in it. Amelia Russell said of him: " He was æsthetic in his ideas, and perhaps studied beauty a little more than profit." He died poor in California, where he went during the gold fever.

Among the women who gave loyally of their strength, a few besides Mrs. Sophia Ripley, Mrs. Mary (Bullard) Dwight, and Mrs. Orvis, who are best commemorated with their husbands, deserve a word because of their special charm or capability. Miss Amelia Russell, whose two papers in the *Atlantic Monthly* are conspicuous for good judgment and for accuracy, was known as " Mistress of the Revels," playing an important part in the Amusement Group, of which she was long the chief, because of her skill in arranging the various games and theatrical efforts. She also taught dancing, and achieved an honest fame as the clear starcher *par excellence* of the Association. One of the children, in recognition of her abilities as a laundress, called her "Miss Muslin." She had good manners, a petite and engaging personality, and was, as her writing shows, a woman of cultivation and tolerant mind. It is noteworthy that on her arrival she met with the same peculiar reception accorded, no one knows why, to others, who have mentioned the experience. No one spoke to her, although she had previously seen some of the members. "They kept about their occupations, utterly regardless of me." Lizzie Curson, who came from Newburyport, was not one of the celebrities, but she is of gracious memory for her untiring fidelity as chief for more than two years of the Dormitory Group. She was skilled in the art of housing for the night unexpected comers, and met the perplexities of her task with uniform serenity. She became the wife of John Andrews Hoxie, a carpenter at Brook Farm, and died a year or two ago. Mrs. Almira Barlow, who lived in a front room of the Hive with her three boys, had been a Miss Penniman, a famous beauty in Brookline, and of a lively and attractive disposition.   Later the Curtis brothers were her fast friends in Concord, where for a time they all found themselves.   The impression, if a wrong one, is hard to escape, that Hawthorne may have had this lady's personal fascinations in mind when he drew certain characteristics of his Zenobia.

George Ripley and Sophia Willard Ripley   The ranks of reformers are seldom recruited by so unprejudiced and candid a mind as that of George Ripley.   From the beginning to the close of his anxious but not unquiet life, his judgment controlled his passions, and he could discern the truth with clearness even when knowledge of the truth meant the loss of everything but courage and ideals.

Ripley's first serious disappointment had been his failure to build up the Unitarian parish in Boston, which had been gathered for him on his leaving the Harvard Divinity School.   His friends had felt no doubt that his personality and unusual intellectual equipment would awaken the spiritual life of a large neighborhood.   Alas, for the drawing qualities of sincerity and personal piety!   They were no more potent in 1826 at the corner of Pearl and Purchase streets than they are to-day in correspondingly respectable quarters — after the newness was somewhat worn away.

For more than fourteen years Ripley's ministrations went faithfully on.   He was often tried by the limitations put upon his speech by the traditions of his profession, and by the failure of his parishioners to take any deep interest in what seemed to him some of the most vital concerns of human life ; and finally, in October, 1840, he wrote from Northampton to his people, the manliest of letters, setting forth, with absolute open-mindedness, the incompatibilities which were separating him from them.   The letter was accepted by the Purchase Street parish as a convincing argument.   They, too, saw the futility of a longer attempt to engender a spiritual glow where there seemed to be neither tinder nor ignitible material; and the minister preached his farewell sermon on March 28, 1841, to a somewhat sorrowful but not afflicted people.

Although Ripley was a philosopher he was not visionary ; he could not deceive himself any more than he could another man.   Perhaps, next to his love for truth, his strongest characteristic was caution ; but having patiently convinced himself of the righteousness of a course of conduct, he pursued it until he was equally certain that he had made a mistake.   A full decade was consumed in discerning the impossibility of harmonizing Christian doctrine and Christian life under existing social conditions, and in forming the resolution to establish, if he could, better conditions.

So far as a man of Ripley's intellectual can-

K

dor can be influenced by other minds, it is probable that he was swayed by the talk and the writing of Dr. Hedge. The latter had been one of his revered instructors in the Divinity School, and had published in the *Christian Examiner* of March, 1833, an article on Coleridge, which recorded the great results flowing from the spread of Schelling's ideal philosophy. This naturally strengthened the set of Ripley's thought, already turned into this channel. It would be impossible, though interesting, to trace the growth of the Brook Farm scheme in his mind. One fact, however, is beyond dispute: Ripley sacrificed his personal feelings in pushing the enterprise. He wrote to Emerson: "Personally, my tastes and habits would lead me in another direction. I have a passion of being independent of the world, and of every man in it. This I could do easily on the estate which is now offered, which I could rent at a rate that, with my other resources, would place me in a very agreeable condition so far as my personal interests were involved — I should hope one day to drive my own cart to market and sell greens."

While Ripley's project clearly did not gain the sanction of several of his warmest personal friends, it was not seriously opposed by them. Ripley was, at this time, thirty-eight years of age, with a reputation for unusual mental balance, and it was quite impossible that he should

make so serious a move through mere enthusiasm for practising what he preached. Everybody who knew him felt assured that his eyes
were wide open to the practical obstacles, and
that he saw the resources with which to meet
them. On that side his friends trusted him.
What they doubtless feared was, perhaps, best
expressed by Margaret Fuller, who wrote to
William Henry Channing: "His mind, though
that of a captain, is not that of a conqueror."
Nobody would have admitted this more freely
than Ripley himself. He had early realized
that he possessed neither the taste nor the temperament for the rôle of a popular leader; while
yet a student he had written to his mother:
"I am not one of those who can write or speak
from the inspiration of genius, but all that I do
must be the result of my own personal, untiring
efforts"; and he certainly felt that, in the long
run, any mode of life which was at once right and
feasible, although novel, would commend itself
to general society whether backed by a "conqueror" or by a level-headed man who was more
ready even to work than to "lead." If one
were to mention a single quality which Ripley
mostly lacked and which would have stood him
in better stead even, at this time, than his knowledge of practical affairs, it would be worldly
wisdom. Although this quality is not a common accompaniment of idealism, the two are

not by any means irreconcilable. The almost universal verdict has been that the Brook Farm experiment was untimely; and yet a "timelier" time certainly could not have been pitched upon, so far as the condition of public feeling was concerned. If there had been no Brook Farm, there would have been something else. The ferment in men's minds must somewhere and somehow have thrown something to the surface of society; and there is the keenest satisfaction to-day in the assurance that this hunger and thirst after social righteousness could not have found a nobler expression, even if it could have found a wiser one. At all events, George Ripley was irrevocably committed to associative co-operation — a social ideal which his wife, Sophia Ripley, accepted with even more outward enthusiasm than he himself. The unqualified support of so fine a spirit as Sophia Ripley might well strengthen conviction, and George Ripley had been buoyed up by it too long already not to know its full value.

The first weeks at Brook Farm were full for these leaders of the enterprise. The farm must be made ready for cultivation, and the domestic machinery set in motion; and the interminable detail of all this naturally fell very largely on the Ripleys. With their customary honesty they had set before themselves and before their friends the weary months — perhaps years —

during which the process of establishing their
project should demand all their strength and
return to them only the most meagre rewards.
In his younger days Ripley had felt "pretty
well satisfied that he should be happier in the
city than he could ever be in the country";
but as his theory of the wholesomeness of combined manual and intellectual work developed,
this preference for city life gave way. Gleefully he donned the farmer's blouse, the wide
straw hat, and the high boots in which he has
been pictured at Brook Farm; and whether he
cleaned stables, milked cows, carried vegetables
to market, and estimated probable crops from
improbable soil in the morning, or taught
philosophy and mathematics and discussed
religion with Parker (who called him the
"Archon") in the afternoon, or led the brilliant
conversations in the common parlor in the evening — he gave the same conscientious thought
to all. The mere matter of correspondence
must often have been looked upon as a
weary necessity, and yet the answers to both
sincere and insincere "inquirers" were unfail-
ingly kind. This courtesy never forsook him,
and his constant good temper and good cheer
have been the occasion of almost universal
comment among the members of a society in
which both were far more common than is
usual. He was one of the few men whom

Abigail Folsom, the "flea of conventions," could not irritate. The humbler the task the better it suited Ripley; it gave him, for instance, the purest joy to black William Allen's boots for him before the latter went to Boston. His self-control was of the sort that sends a jest to the lips when anxiety presses heavily on the heart, and marked, in his case, not so much force of will as of character. The nature of the only apparent impediment to success — lack of money — must have been peculiarly harassing. That a few thousand dollars should stand between disaster and an ensured future has shattered much lofty zeal on the part of idealists who scorn so vulgar a means of access to paradise.

Mr. Ripley, however, had no words of reproach for people who were slow to invest in a project which showed no sign of return, although it is fair to suppose that he had hoped that more people would be willing to run risks in the matter; and to-day it seems not a little singular that in the midst of the shrill popular cry for a higher life, financial support should not have been offered by certain men and women whose hearts at least indorsed this attempt. Undiscouraged, then, to all outward appearance, the chief organizer and promoter of Brook Farm walked unhesitatingly on, conscious before many months had passed that the path which he had chosen led along a dangerous and probably impassable way. At the end of two years the question of industrial organization became a common topic of discussion and in the first months of 1844 such a step for Brook Farm was decided upon. It is not wholly clear through what processes Ripley reached his decision in this matter; for a more fundamental change in his attitude regarding what was socially desirable, he could not have made. It must have been that he came to lay more stress on the method by which individual freedom was to become assured, than on the fact of personal liberty in itself. He had agreed, up to this time, that the possibility of guaranteeing to every man the opportunity to develop himself into a symmetrical being could only be gained through the least necessary organization; but since unorganized society clearly was not calling out, in point of numbers, the membership essential to the stability of any civilized society, and since Fourier's elaboration did away with the chief stumbling block to the highest personal liberty — competition — why not Fourierism? It was only another marked instance of Ripley's disposition to accept the truth when he believed he had found it, let it clash ever so fiercely with his tastes and desires. The decision made prodigious demands upon him; for in urging the adoption of this system he felt strongly the responsibility which he had laid on himself of bringing it into successful operation. He wrote and lectured with unceasing fervor in the faith that wide popular knowledge would ultimately convince those who were worthy to be received into a higher social order.

It is not pertinent to dwell here on the paradoxes of the New England conscience ; but we may remind ourselves that just as the strongest religious faith in certain races bears no clear relation to their moral sense, so the New England heart and mind have been eternally at odds. The compromise which they have effected is this : the hard head, holding dominion over the soft heart, regulates conduct and keeps at a safe distance from doubtful investments, while allowing the heart unlimited sympathy with every good cause.

When, in the fall of 1845, the money was raised for finishing the unitary building, hope reassumed, for a time, its commanding position. How short-lived was this renewed vision of attainment has already been told, and, although Ripley's outward serenity varied not an appreciable hair from the normal, he realized almost immediately the bitter significance of the Phalanstery fire. He knew that the expectation of any considerable financial assistance was now futile, but he could meet this knowledge with a smile which betokened that his faith in a principle was far deeper than any disappointment. Not that he abated a whit, even then, his consecrated labor, for his energy did not flag, and his determination to obey the promptings of duty or love — since they were synonymous terms in his vocabulary — did not falter; but he had heard the hour strike. A little later in the year his best intellectual solace, his library, was sold to Theodore Parker, to pay certain debts of the Phalanx. This treasured possession was largely responsible for Ripley's broad and well-grounded scholarship, his unprejudiced and impersonal view of men and of letters, and his unalterable devotion to the intuitive philosophy. His books numbered many French and German works on ethics, philosophy, and biblical criticism, besides much miscellaneous material in the domain of pure literature; and only he who has given up what has become a part of his intellectual self, knows the wrench which this necessity was to Ripley. As he took a last look at these victims of his failure, he said: "I can now understand how a man would feel if he could attend his own funeral."

The transfer of the property to a board of trustees was made in August, 1847, and the office of the *Harbinger* having been removed to New York, the Ripleys followed, making their home in Flatbush, Long Island. Mr. Ripley continued his editorial labors, with indifferent encouragement, for something less than two years, when, after an illness of several weeks, his convalescence was greeted by the discovery that the *Harbinger* had ceased to be. Dust and emptiness were the only occupants of the little room in the top of the old *Tribune* building.

Employment was at once offered him on the *Tribune*, although at first it seems to have been irregular and unprofitable. He earned $38 by his contribution to that paper between May 5 and July 14, 1849, an average of $3.80 a week. Not until September 21, 1851, did he receive a regular salary of $25 a week. From this point his fortunes gradually brightened until January 11, 1871, when it was agreed to pay him $75 a week. In the meantime he had moved to New York City, and in addition to his *Tribune* work, his articles added occasional strength to the columns of at least a dozen magazines; but the greatest monument to his industry and ability was the "American Cyclopædia," which was the project of Dr. Hawks, and which, in 1857, was undertaken with Ripley and Dana as editors. The first edition was completed in 1862, and it represented, for the first time, perhaps, a successful attempt at historical, political, and ecclesiastical impartiality on an encyclopædic scale.

After a painful illness Mrs. Ripley died from

a cancer, in February, 1861. Her husband made every effort to alleviate her weeks of suffering; but at the time he was receiving twenty-five dollars a week from the *Tribune*, and the Ripleys were living in one room. His distress of mind for her sake over cramped conditions was no less intense because it could not be inferred from his calm exterior.

Mrs. Ripley's life and work had been so intimately associated with her husband's that it seems fitting at this point to consider her part in the history of Brook Farm, although her service was quite important enough to be treated by itself. Sophia Willard Dana, the daughter of Francis Dana of Cambridge, married George Ripley in 1827. The previous year he had written home of the "being whose influence over me for the year past has so much elevated, strengthened, and refined my character"; and he had added that his regard for Miss Dana was "founded not upon any romantic or sudden passion, but upon great respect for intellectual power, moral worth, deep and true Christian piety, and peculiar refinement and dignity of character." Mrs. Ripley was in complete accord with her husband on all vital questions, but her temperament differed so radically from his that although she met opposition with as much courage as he, she showed less forbearance than he to the opposer. Ardor and impulsiveness were strong in her, but they were only the superficial expression of deep feeling and not substitutes for it. Her sympathies were wide and deep, but they were hardly so all-embracing as were her husband's. Gifted in mind and brilliant in conversation, it is easy to credit the tradition that her somewhat impetuous espousal of the community idea deeply annoyed her family and friends; the ready delight with which she exchanged the duties of a minister's wife for those of a maid-of-all-work might properly be expected to scandalize a conservative Cambridge family in any age. The first shock, of course, wore off, and when, later, the chief of the Wash-room Group was occasionally persuaded to seek a brief diversion among her Boston or Cambridge friends, her folly was generously overlooked and she received much pleasant social attention. She was a tall and graceful woman, slight in figure, and fair in coloring. She was near-sighted, but she depended on glasses only when looking at distant objects.

Her power of infusing life into those around her must have been extraordinary, and no amount of fatigue or discouragement seemed to affect it. Like her husband, she was always eager to undertake the most distasteful employments—such as the continuous nursing, for some little time, of the young Manila leper, Lucas Cor-

rales. Indeed, as Miss Russell, her warm friend
and admirer, has said: " Impossible seemed a
word unknown to her."   The eight or ten hours
a day which she at first spent on laundry work
were later modified, because her skill as a teacher
brought her more and more into demand in the
school; but it is said that she managed, apparently without the least effort, to impart to the
laundry a constant atmosphere of almost seduc-
tive cheerfulness.   One of the Associates says
that she lacked " nature," and was wholly in-
competent to advise or influence, in important
emergencies, vigorous, natural young persons
not on her plane of thought.   This may be true,
but it is equivalent to saying that nobody understood everybody, even in a society where so
much was held in common.

There is some doubt as to the warmth of Mrs.
Ripley's convictions regarding the expansion of
Brook Farm into a Phalanx.   When the first
interest in Fourier showed itself in the community, she wrote : " I am greatly drawn of late
to a close study of Fourier. His science of
Association recommends itself more and more
to my feelings and conscience, and I am constrained to accept him as a man of genius, a
discoverer; though I believe that in many things
his system is to be modified by the spirit of our
times and nation."   Whatever the spirit in
which she accepted the new policy, there was

no visible sign of disappointment — only the
old courage and buoyancy. When, however,
disaster really came, her strength failed; and
the consolation that George Ripley found in the
contemplation of a heroic fight in which defeat
had left his ideals untouched, she sought in that
church which offers to make secure the future
of any soul which submits to its discipline.   One
can only guess how much the closing of a common channel of sympathy affected Ripley; but
he could not have been indifferent to the
shutting off of a great field of thought and
feeling in which they had hitherto walked in
harmony.

Mrs. Ripley taught for some time after the
move to New York, and became gradually absorbed in charitable and philanthropic work.
The household was still a happy one, each taking the same genuine interest in the other's
work, but there was always the forbidden
ground on which neither cared to venture.
Thus more than a decade passed before the
fatality which terminated Sophia Ripley's life.
After her death Ripley went to Brooklyn, and
perhaps, as never before, gave way to grief.
But his healthy nature could not long entertain
morbidness, and he returned to New York, to
take up again his normal and busy life.   His
second marriage in the fall of 1865 with Mrs.
Schlossberger, a German lady some thirty years

his junior, who married again after his death, brought him many years of wholesome companionship — years, too, which, though far from idle, were lightened by intervals of rest and travel. From April until October, 1866, he was in Europe, and it was during this visit that he paid a memorable call recently described by Justin McCarthy. Armed with a letter of introduction from Emerson, he sought Carlyle, who had once described him as "a Socinian minister who left his pulpit in order to reform the world by cultivating onions." Ripley listened patiently to a long and violent tirade against the conduct of the Federal government in America, but he made no effort to stem the torrent of Carlyle's wrath. When the noisy silentiary paused for a moment, — a rare occurrence, — Ripley quietly gathered himself up, and without a word of remonstrance left the Chelsea home, not again to cross its threshold. His second visit to Europe covered the time from May, 1869, to the fall of 1870, and in the course of these months he sent to the *Tribune* some remarkable letters on the Franco-Prussian War, and an able and fair-minded criticism on the proceedings of the Ecumenical Council which assembled at the Vatican in 1870. Like his friend Parker, Ripley had no great love for art or for natural beauty, and his attention while abroad was almost wholly absorbed by the consideration of peoples, institutions, and social problems.

Some of the most important writing which Ripley had hoped to do, he did not live to accomplish. He left uncompleted the chapter on "Philosophic Thought in Boston," which he was preparing for the fourth volume of Winsor's "Memorial History." His friend Channing had long been urging him to write a history of modern systems of philosophy — a task for which his extraordinary mental balance especially fitted him, but this he apparently had not even begun. George Bancroft wrote with regret that a history of intellectual culture in Boston did not come from Ripley's pen, "for he has left us no one who can write it so justly, so tenderly, and with such knowledge of the subject and candor and skill as he would have done."

As a young man Ripley was slender, with a pale, clean-shaven face, closely curling brown hair, and black eyes which were so near-sighted that he always wore spectacles. In later life he grew stout and wore a beard, and the vision of the "formal, punctilious, ascetic" young clergyman of the early forties was replaced by that of the cheerful, scholarly man of the world of the early seventies — an appearance that he maintained to the time of his death on July 4, 1880.

Ripley discharged all the obligations resting on the Brook Farm Phalanx at the time of its dissolution. Although these did not amount to more than one thousand dollars, the last receipt was dated December 22, 1862, and was an acknowledgment of payment, partly in money and partly by a copy of the "Cyclopædia," received for groceries. No sharper comment is necessary on the deprivations of his first years in New York. It has been felt that nobody gained less from the Brook Farm experiment than did Ripley, and although that surmise must in many ways be true, it cannot, in the largest sense, be accepted by those who have followed carefully the man's after life. The blows of the hammer may harden the metal into a rail or temper it into a Damascus blade. Both the bludgeon and the blade are useful, but the latter does the finer work. So when courage becomes not defiance but fortitude; when endurance does not allow itself to sink into stoicism at the death of that in which belief has been deepest, there is good certainty that much besides a crushing impact has accrued to the victim of fate.

Some of the nicknames foisted on the various Associates seem forced and even witless, but the "Professor" was no bad title for Dana. Born at Hinsdale, New Hampshire, in 1819, he passed his boyhood in Buffalo and there worked in a store, and fitted himself

Charles Anderson Dana

L

for Harvard College, which he entered in 1839.
When he was in the middle of his course his
sight became seriously weakened from reading
"Oliver Twist" by candle light. At three in
the morning he had finished the badly printed
volume, and had nearly ruined his eyes. Several
Harvard men were already at Brook Farm, and
they invited Dana to join them. He went
thither in the fall of 1841 to begin his work in
the school as an instructor in Greek and German. He received his degree from Harvard
College in 1863 as of the class of 1843, and
from the same college the honorary degree of
Master of Arts in 1861.

Dana seems not to have defied worldly custom
either in the matter of blouses or unusual hair;
in fact, he was not especially responsive to
the little caprices of his fellows, and seldom
joined in the merriment, but was always on
hand for the serious affairs, having been made
a trustee soon after his arrival. He not only
worked and taught well, but sang well, and was
bass in a choir, which, according to Arthur Sumner, sang a "Kyrie Eleison" night and day. "It
seems to me," adds Sumner, "that they sang it
rather often." One admirable bit of training for
his future profession Dana acquired through his
connection with the *Harbinger*, to which he was
a frequent contributor. Many of his articles
were youthful and imitative—hardly better than

any well brought-up young fellow might produce. The mannerisms of the sturdy English reviewing of the day sat heavily upon him, and he was constantly dismissing the victims of his disapproval with the familiar congé of the British quarterlies. Short poems and literary notices formed the major part of his work, but it is unnecessary to particularize the amount or quality of what he did. It was all excellent practice. Poe, Cooper, and Anthon were his youthful hatreds.

According to Colonel Higginson the Professor was "the best all-round man at Brook Farm, but was held not to be quite so zealous or unselfish for the faith as were some of the others," though his speeches in Boston and elsewhere were most effective. Dana was at that time a very young man, with the faults, but with all the splendor and promise of youth. No one has criticised the fidelity of his work at the school, and no one, not excepting Ripley, spoke more fervidly than Dana in the cause of Association. He was wise, if not wholly ingenuous, for he had the sagacity at the meeting held in December, 1843, to advocate a continuance of Associationism for Brook Farm, while the followers of Brisbane, bringer of huge programmes and unnumbered woes, proclaimed the virtues of modified Fourierism. Dana lost the toss, but did not forsake the field. On the contrary, even after the flames of the Phalanstery swept up vortically the hopes of five years, he still valiantly preached the faith delivered to the saints. As a mature man the great editor found so few causes on which he could lavish his vanishing enthusiasm that it is a pleasure to recall his scrupulous adhesion to the doctrines of Association until those doctrines became normally merged into vaster and more immediate problems. His name ranks in importance with Orvis and Allen as a lecturer, although he probably did not, so often as they, address the public. But when he talked he was influential. On the platform Dana had no especial fluency, but he did have the compensating graces of frankness and a natural manner. On one occasion he defended, and most honestly, ambition as "the greatest of the four social passions." This it was, the speaker argued, which brought the Associates together in order to better social conditions. It corresponds to the seventh note of music, requiring for completeness the striking of the eighth note, which belongs also to the octave beyond. To strike these notes is to arrive at a final object, the higher unity. Noble and straightforward sentiments, but born, one would hardly think, of that "mordaunt and luminous spirit," as Dana was afterward remembered. In Dana, however, there were memories, some of them tender, for these sincerer days. Dana, who wore no emotions on his sleeve, never forgot, and never in word, however much in conduct, repudiated Brook Farm. No abler or more sympathetic tribute has ever been paid to the Association than was spoken by him at the University of Michigan on January 21, 1895. The charm of the life, the causes of failure, his own experiences, are all candidly and gracefully told. Mr. Ripley is mentioned with respect and cordiality. Where the treasure is there will the heart be also. Charles Dana, who laughed at much which some men hold dear, never vilipended his own experience at Brook Farm, though it is a matter of conjecture whether he retained faith in any particular reform, social or political. He took pains in this lecture to deny that there was any communism in the experiment. Nothing in his nature would have responded to that principle. The real trouble at Brook Farm to him was evident: "it didn't pay"; but he insisted that the breaking up was regretted by all who shared the life there. He severed his own connection soon after the fire, at which he did not chance to be present, and secured work in Boston on the *Chronotype* at five dollars a week.

He joined the staff of the *Tribune* in 1847, and in 1848 went to Europe as a correspondent of five papers, — an early instance of syndicate letter-writing, — and earned thereby about forty

dollars a week. This lasted for eight months,
when he returned to the *Tribune*, on the staff of
which he remained until Greeley, who disagreed
with Dana over the conduct of the war, dis-
missed him in 1862. He was made a special
commissioner of the War Department to look
after the condition of the pay service in the
West, and was confirmed as Assistant Secretary
of War in January, 1864. For reasons of personal safety he had also been appointed by
Secretary Stanton, in June, 1863, an assistant
adjutant general with the rank of major. At
the front for purposes of closer observation, and
associated in Washington with the men who
surrounded Lincoln and his cabinet, Dana's
ability had the fullest opportunity to declare itself. In 1865 he took charge of the newly
started *Chicago Republican*, but in 1868 issued
his first number of the *New York Sun*, of which
for nearly thirty years thereafter he was the essential force, though always supported by a staff
conspicuous in the ranks of American journalism.

When Dana forsook the isolation of Brook
Farm, he found many shining examples of a
pretentiousness which he genuinely despised.
A good hater with an early start, a critic without
careful balance, it was natural enough that he
should soon find himself in contact with a vast
deal of humbug. It was not difficult for him,
with his temper, to begin to find that his oppo-

nents were charlatans, or at least that they had sufficient duplicity to make him distrust them. The theory is a convenient one : it is easier to distrust a man because you dislike him, than to dislike him because you distrust him. Mr. Dana was ready at finding motives for vindictive hatred toward men who did not do what pleased him. He met the fate of all who do not cherish the spirit of fairness : he continued to interest and to please, but his judgment was discredited. There are many who can bear testimony to the generosity and helpfulness of Dana, especially toward men of his profession ; his private life, his refinements and tastes were irreproachable. Many good men had no faith in him, and thought him to have been false and unsubstantial. Other men, who stood near him, are willing to affirm that on a question of principle he never ratted. However all this may be, in the judgment of those who best knew Brook Farm, he, of all its associates, departed furthest from its aspirations.

Dana was accounted a handsome man, not after the graceful type of the Curtises, but masculine, yet so slender as to seem tall. He had a firm, expressive face, regular and clear cut, a scholar's forehead, auburn hair, and a full beard. Strong in mind and general physique, he conveyed the impression of force whether he moved or spoke. In his old age he preserved a look of virility and determination, though hard-headedness clearly predominated over gracious-ness. He was, at Brook Farm, kindly mannered, and gave a pleasant impression to those who met him, while a natural dignity kept him from many of the extravagances into which some of the others easily fell. He showed a taste for the farm work, which later, when success gave opportunity, grew into a fondness for livestock and all the accompaniments of a country life. An admirable nervous and muscular strength explains much of Dana's capacity for successful work.

A Southern family at Brook Farm, by the name of Macdaniel, consisted of a mother, two daughters, Fanny and Eunice, and a son, Osborne. Eunice became the wife of Dana while they were at the Farm, though the wedding did not take place on the estate. Maria Dana, Charles Dana's sister, married Osborne Macdaniel, who wrote a number of articles, strong but eccentric, for the *Harbinger*. Macdaniel was of a deeply speculative turn of mind, but did not hold that philosophy was adapted to everyday life. Mrs. Macdaniel, whose mentality is as vigorous as was her brother's, has never abandoned the faith.

It is not a cheerful prospect to face

John Sullivan
Dwight

existence as a stickit minister; but it was inevitable for a man who, through excess of feeling and want of assertiveness, wept on the occasion of reading his first marriage service. To underestimate a man thus dowered is easy. Parker, mistaking essential gentleness for fundamental weakness, assured Dwight that impulse assumed the place of will in his character, and that he lacked "Selbstständigkeit." Lowell, too, seems to have been hardly more accurate in his interpretation of Dwight, for as late as 1854 he committed the amusing *bêtise* of suggesting that Dwight's proper career might be the establishment of a "bureau for governesses."

It was natural that John Dwight should turn fondly to West Roxbury, for it was once the home of his mother, Mary Corey. He was himself a Boston boy, the son of Dr. John Dwight; he was a graduate of the Latin School, of Harvard College, and of the Divinity School. A lover of fine letters, the poet of his class at Harvard at graduation (1832), he also found or made time to devote himself to music. He was a member of the Pierian Sodality, an organization which still maintains repute in the undergraduate activities, and his zeal for music continued during his course at the Divinity School, from which he was graduated in 1836. The frequent experience of a university career was his: that the main objects of his training were gradually lost in the development of stronger interests. The promising academic scholar and the young Unitarian cleric were soon, but not too speedily,

absorbed in the teacher and critic of music,
later to dominate opinion in a large community
for many years.   He was one of the first members of a society formed in 1837, which as early
as 1840 had taken the permanent name of the
" Harvard Musical Association," and which in
a few years exerted an influence far beyond the
institution which gave it name and habitation.

It is not clear why Dwight ever wished to be
a preacher ; religious he may easily have been,
but theology was not in him.   Miss Elizabeth
Peabody once spoke to him frankly of a " certain want of fluency in prayer," and Theodore
Parker, who roomed near him as a divinity student, was not reluctant seemingly to point out a
vagueness which " mistook the indefinite for the
Infinite."   His one important ministry was at
Northampton, where he preached during a part
of 1839, and where he was ordained in the
spring of 1840.   At the close of this episode,
in the summer of 1841, he withdrew from the
profession, though he occasionally " assisted "
Channing at the meetings of the Associationists
in Boston some years later.   He did not, like
Channing, vibrate between the pulpit and socialistic schemes, but stepped definitely out into the
arena of the Newness.   The disruption was not
violent, and little sense of disappointment or
failure was evident on his part.   Retreat with
him never meant surrender, and he did not as-

cribe to loss of faith a change made compulsory by his own lack of fitness for one of the professions.

Dwight came to Brook Farm without kindred, although his parents and two sisters joined him later and remained with him. He was young, unmarried, and well rid of the mournful obligation of earning a living through a calling from which the zest was gone; but he did not enter the experiment because there was no opening elsewhere, though to be sure his capital stock was mainly a lofty enthusiasm. Not until November of the first year of the Farm did he become a member of the Association, and to him was soon assigned, in the school, the work of instruction in music and Latin. Resourcefulness is, after all, an admirable test of ability, and Dwight, starting his new career with a fair education and some aptitude for imparting his knowledge, quickly developed his greatest capacity and instilled into the whole community his own conceptions regarding music. The other influences of Brook Farm were indirect; but John Dwight, diffident and seclusive as he was, imposed on the Association a cult which formed no part of the original programme outside the school curriculum.

Though he might come to his task, which he loved, tired with the work on the farm, which he barely endured, he felt that this alternation of

drudgeries was good for him. In later years
he said: " I have no doubt I should not have
been living at this day if it had not been for the
life there, for what I did on the farm and among
the trees, in handling the hay, and even in
handling the scythe." Tradition does not say
how close any one dared to approach when a
Transcendentalist swung so lethal an implement
as the scythe; but cautious beholders would have
been justified in maintaining that prudent remoteness observed by Longfellow, who declined
to go into the wilds when he learned that
Emerson had purchased a gun for the expedi-
tion.

Mr. George Willis Cooke, from whose interesting volume on Dwight many facts here given
are gratefully drawn, has compared Dwight's
influence at this period to that of Emerson,
Parker, and Ripley. If " Einfluss " is to be insisted upon, and the transplantation of German
ideas to be held of much account in the simple
story of Boston Transcendentalism, the name of
Beethoven must enter any reckoning which includes Goethe and Kant. No external influence
has been so potent or lasting in Boston as the
genuine love for Beethoven, and for the few
other names clustering about the greater
genius.

Literary work was one of Dwight's minor
interests in his West Roxbury life, although he

had earlier tried his hand with some success at such employment. During his clerical career he had taken a modest part in the brisk interest which had arisen in favor of German studies. He translated a considerable part of and edited the whole of the "Select Minor Poems of Goethe and Schiller" for the second volume of Ripley's "Specimens of Foreign Standard Literature." The book was inscribed to Carlyle, who showed himself wonderfully gracious in giving permission for the dedication; but he warned Dwight against "the thrice accursed sin of self-conceit." Dwight was still in Northampton when the first number of the *Dial* appeared, to the first volume of which he contributed several articles, among them his poem called " Rest," which to this day passes current as a translation from Goethe The last four verses, —

> " 'Tis loving and serving
> The Highest and Best!
> 'Tis onward! unswerving,
> And that is true rest," —

might well have been written by the hand that so largely guided an earlier exaltation, and might, oddly enough, have been set over, with an added ethical note, by Carlyle. It is a curious instance not only of powerful influence but of an impersonal fame.

Dwight assisted in editing the *Harbinger*, and

his contributions, though limited in range, were
not narrow, and showed an evident aim at catho-
licity.   The directness of his criticisms — for to
these his efforts were mainly confined — had a
touch of modernness; he was altogether sincere
and showed little trace of influence, and herein
his work manifested an essential superiority
over that of Dana in the same periodical.   He
seldom deliberately tried to be clever, but allowed the natural sweetness of his mind to
diffuse itself.   The pepperiness of which he
was fully capable came later, after he had become something of a Nestor in musical judgment; but even then he did not manifest it
temperamentally.   Only when the necessity
arose for giving expression to a profound conviction of what he felt to be wrong principles in
art did this quality come to the front.

The firmness of his beliefs sometimes passed
from determination into obstinacy, and he enjoyed a well-earned though not evil reputation
for being "set."   He was the central figure of
a little story which passed from mouth to mouth,
until Emerson put it into print, without, however, naming Dwight.   Mr. Ripley said to
Theodore Parker: "There is your accomplished
friend; he would hoe corn all Sunday if I would
let him, but all Massachusetts could not make him
do it on Monday."   Rumor adds that Parker replied: "It is good to know that he wants to hoe

corn any day in the week." One who knew him well says that Dwight was something of a quiddle, which is not so dangerous an appellation as it looks to the unacquainted eye, and which means only that he was fussy over trifles, in the same way in which the Englishman of popular legend is supposed to comport himself in relation to his tub when travelling. Dwight was not fond of excessive toil, and did his work just about when and how he pleased. This, it is said, is one reason why Ditson was obliged to discontinue the publishing of the *Journal of Music*. If Dwight set his own measure for work, he could not fairly have been called slothful; but he worked in the spirit of a dilettante — he indulged his moods, or, perhaps better, respected them.

As is often possible with fine organizations, he was able to adapt himself sympathetically to all conditions, mental and social. His nature was too large for a show of fastidiousness. He bore out the fact that only a gentleman can be a true democrat. His ideals were soaring, but he made it an obligation to be entirely human at the daily task, and in the schoolroom; at the table, especially, he was of a whole-souled simplicity, and a good companion of the hour. He even punned, and punned exceeding ill.

The younger members of the Brook Farm family called him the "Poet," more in recog-

nition of his temperament than of his verse —
none of which has been widely remembered,
except the seven stanzas, "Rest," already alluded to. Only a poet, however, such as the
young folks thought him, would have proposed
to leave the Association, with the liberty of an
occasional return, in order to earn more money
which he would turn back into the community.
This was lofty, but it was not visionary. John
Dwight was by no means indisposed to the comfort and warmth of this world, idealist as he unquestionably was. He loved books, art, friends;
he even loved good dinners. During a visit to
New York, where he delivered some lectures
just after the Phalanstery fire, Dwight diligently
sought aid for the falling venture; but it was too
late, although he did not seem fully to realize
the fact. The curtain is wisely drawn over the
last days of Brook Farm. Ripley and Dwight,
who kindled the fires and fanned them to a
steady flame, were not the men to feel the chill
as the embers burned low. But at last there
was little need to remain over the ashes unless
they would remain alone. The willingness to
leave Brook Farm temporarily for the sake of
the cause found its natural complement in the
fact that Dwight was slow to desert it at the
last, remaining even after Ripley had gone.

It was fitting that, in 1851, W. H. Channing
should join in marriage Mary Bullard and John

Dwight, both of them connected, he directly, she as a visitor, with Brook Farm, and both Associationists in Boston. This union was a happy and in every sense a suitable one, and it represented one of the brightest results of the tendency at Brook Farm to bring together harmonious minds. Of several worthy marriages traceable to the days of the Association none was more propitious than that of Dwight and Mary Bullard, of whom Channing said that she was the most thoroughly conscientious person he ever knew. Their capital was love and good courage, for Dwight was still without certainties for the future. He wrote for Elizur Wright's *Chronotype*, a one-cent paper published in Boston. Dana, Brisbane, Cranch, and the two cousins Channing, also assisted in this venture, which did not, however, succeed. Neither music nor reform languished with Dwight; he wrote in his especial field for journals in New York and Philadelphia, and was musical editor of the *Boston Commonwealth*. *Dwight's Journal of Music* first appeared under the date of April 10, 1852. The editor wrote to Cranch, a contributor to the first number: "It is my last, desperate (no very confident) grand *coup d'état* to try and get a living." Back of the enterprise stood the faithful Harvard Musical Association, and there was no lack of good will and personal effort on the part of Dwight's

M

friends, most of whom were, like himself, still in the tentative period of life. The first year paid for itself; but the *Journal* was as uncompromising as the *Liberator*, which appealed to the wider sentiments of humanity and justice, and subsistence is likely to be an actual problem for a man who writes without the spirit of conciliation and who has not the least faculty for seizing an opportunity to enrich himself, should such an opportunity come. Twelve hundred dollars a year was the value set on this idealist in his palmiest days, but probably as many cents would have satisfied him, could he, on that sum, have maintained his self-respect. Since he cared little for popularity, there is an interesting suggestion in the fact that Dwight's very lack of technical discrimination and his persistent adherence to simplicity and grandeur as constant ideals, brought forward and upward the mass of musical opinion. Dwight could, however, be tolerant, though it was easy to discern the effort, as in the case of Wagner, whom he did not and could not like.

After something less than ten years of sympathetic companionship and love, Mary his wife died while he was abroad. It was characteristic of his fineness that he could find it possible to stay his year out in Europe, instead of hurrying back to greater loneliness. The relations of time and space being henceforth disturbed for him, he found her presence as real far from her lonely grave as near it. Thereafter Dwight's home was in the hearts and at the houses of his many friends. He lived, however, after 1873, in the rooms of the Harvard Musical Association — the veritable "genius loci."

On September 3, 1881, appeared the last issue of *Dwight's Journal of Music*, which for thirty years had contended, not without a measure of recognition, for the best conceivable standards. In his old age, therefore, Dwight manfully laid down the task which he had taken up in his prime "to make a living." But he renounced nothing — absolutely nothing. As he thought and wrote in 1850, so did he think and write in 1880. "If one have anything worth saying, will it not be as good to-morrow as to-day?" What he was in the Brook Farm days he remained, — poor, brave, inspiring, intellectually honest. There was no element of calculation in his nature, and therefore it was possible for him honorably to accept assistance, as he occasionally did, from friends who loved him and believed in him ; but such aid was rendered rather to his cause than to the man himself. To be helped in this way, without loss of self-respect, is a test of dignity, though the experiment is necessarily dangerous. Dwight's character suffered no loss ; it even gained in serenity. He dispensed such kindness as he could, and is remembered for his good will toward young musicians. He was even able to help, in her failing days, an old Brook Farm visitor — Signora Biscaccianti. His face was kindly, and his manner gentle to those whom he knew. He was of short stature, his head was a fine one, and in his later years he was of dignified appearance.

Nearly four months after he was eighty years of age, on September 5, 1893, he died. This event brought together such men and women as never gather except to do honor to those who die tenacious of ideals, though profiting nothing from the maintenance thereof, but a continuing memory in the hearts of the elect; and his funeral service was marked by a cheerfulness and sincerity, which, in their recognition of death, well typified the old Brook Farmer's attitude toward life.

Nathaniel Hawthorne

Hawthorne's deciding motive in joining the enterprise at Brook Farm does not appear; but it is possible that he was glad for a time to go into intellectual retreat when his relation with the Boston Custom House was severed in 1841. The money which he invested, one thousand dollars, was saved from his government earnings. His first entry in his note-books bears the date of April 13, 1841, only a few days after Ripley had begun the experiment.   He arrived in the midst of one of those late spring snowstorms which never fail to impress a New Englander with their unseasonableness, though they are as invariable as the solstices.   If the world gained nothing else from this trip to Arcadia, it at least has the benefit of the early pages of the "Blithedale Romance," in which the narrator arrives at nightfall in the midst of just such a storm. The intimate but fallacious relationship between man and nature, her counterplots against his purposes, are here told with Hawthorne's best power.

Hawthorne was at first possessed of a mighty zeal which lasted well into the summer.   His first bucolic experience was with the famous "transcendental heifer," mistakenly said to have been the property of Margaret Fuller.   The beast was recalcitrant and anti-social, and was finally sent to Coventry by the more docile kine, always to be counted on for moderate conservatism. Her would-be tamer, not wishing to be unjust, refers later to this heifer as having "a very intelligent face" and "a reflective cast of character."   He certainly paid her alleged mistress no such tribute, but thus early let appear his thinly veiled contempt for the high priestess of Transcendentalism.   Even earlier his antagonism toward this eminent woman was strong, if it was not frank, when he wrote: "I was invited to dine at Mr. Bancroft's yesterday with Miss Margaret Fuller, but Providence had given me some business to do, for which I was very thankful."

On April 16 he broke a machine for chopping hay, through very excess of effort, and his remarkable energy then employed itself on a heap of manure. This useful adjunct to the new life he soon began to call his "gold mine," but admits that "a man's soul may as well be buried there as under a pile of money." Presently he writes: "I have milked a cow!" He is pleased with his environment, saying: "The scenery is of a mild and placid character;" and in a letter to his sister Louisa: "This is one of the most beautiful places I ever saw in my life, and as secluded as if it were a hundred miles from any city or village." In the same letter he gleefully boasts that he is transformed into a complete farmer, and the next day adds to his note-book that toil "defiles the hands indeed, but not the soul," and speaks of his calling as a righteous and heaven-blest way of life. Spring advanced and turned to summer, and still Nathaniel Hawthorne moiled on, until suddenly, on August 12, he burst forth in a different but not less rhapsodical strain: "In a little more than a fortnight I shall be free from my bondage — free to enjoy Nature — free to think and feel. . . . Oh, labor is the curse of the world, and nobody can meddle with it without becoming proportionably brutified! Is it a praiseworthy matter that I have spent five golden months in providing food for cows and horses? It is not so." On September 22 he records: "Here I am again. . . . I have a friendlier disposition toward the farm now that I am no longer obliged to toil in its stubborn furrows." Three days later there follows a determination not to "spend the winter here." The happy release from the furrows is easily explained by his election to "two high offices," as he calls them, one as Trustee of the Brook Farm Institute, and the other as Chairman of the Committee of Finance. The community may not have shown much earthly wisdom in this selection, but literature is the richer by several pages at this point in his note-book, where are described places in the close neighborhood grown dear to his isolated heart. He even goes to Brighton with William Allen to buy some little pigs, and only four days later bursts forth into that immortal commentary on a pen of full-grown swine, *mox morituri*. The deep and refreshing humor of these few paragraphs gladden, like rain, the heart of him who reads, and are worth the whole of the "Blithedale Romance," if one is seeking merely to discover the true influence of Brook Farm on Hawthorne. The pig as a literary motive was never more delicately conceived, not even in Stevenson's tribute to his black and reluctantly fertile sow in the "Vailima Letters."

Hawthorne liked a quiet laugh, and made welcome any one who could follow his own moods. Hence his attachment to the undemonstrative Tom Orange, a character remembered to this day in West Roxbury, as much for his own personal traits as by reason of his understandings with the taciturn author who gave him renown. Tradition holds that Orange's widow long resisted the attentions of suitors with the same lofty devotion to deceased greatness as was shown by Sarah Churchill to the memory of John, Duke of Marlborough, though it may be that she had found in marriage more acidulation than is expressed by so inviting a name as Orange. At a picnic on the sixth birthday of Frank Dana a masquerade was held in the grove. Orange was present at this motley fun; and Hawthorne, on whom it left a fantastic impression, speaks of his stolid friend as a "thick-set, sturdy figure, enjoying the fun well enough, yet rather laughing with a perception of the nonsensicalness than at all entering into the spirit of the thing." Irony is not wholly reserved for the disposal of the gods.

From this time until the last entry in his notes the new financier seems frankly to have devoted himself to long and solitary walks, studying the changing colors of autumn, and largely ignoring other reasons for his stay at Brook Farm. He abandoned momentarily his observations of the waning season to concern himself with a psychological analysis of a little seamstress who had just arrived from Boston. She was about seventeen years old — a child in action, yet "with all the prerogatives and liabilities of a woman." There is a faint hint in this young creature of Priscilla in the "Blithedale Romance."

One turns regretfully from these charming comments on the neighboring country, and from one in particular on "an upland swell of our pasture, across the valley of the river Charles." On October 27 he joyfully notes: "Fringed gentians — I found the last, probably, that will be seen this year, growing on the margin of the brook." This is the latest entry which has any place here, and it rounds out an incident in the life of a genius — an incident which began with a strenuous attack on a compost heap, and ended, fitly enough, with a lonely discovery of gentians !

The remoteness which he craved was secured to him somehow, but a man of genius may not wholly escape the solicitudes of the women of his family. His mother and sisters did not take kindly to his vague experimenting ; there is even a suspicion that the work at Brook Farm seemed to them "beneath" his level, and they were at no loss for words to convey their feelings. In particular were they anxious lest he work too hard. " Mother groans over it, wishes you would come home," wrote his sister to the brave ploughman as early as the tenth of May. Then they soon generate fears that he may injure himself in hot weather, without thin clothing. " What is the use of burning your brains out in the sun, when you can do anything better with them?" They hear that he is carrying milk into Boston every morning; and his sister Elizabeth, in happier vein, states her belief that he will spoil the cows, if he try to milk them. Thus did the worthiest of women prove their anxiety lest their admired one in any way lower himself by his unaccountable antics. But Hawthorne had an admirable obstinacy, else he would surely have yielded to such powerful domestic pressure. Sisterly care gave way at last to a genuine burst of sarcasm, when Louisa wrote in August: " It is said you are to do the travelling in Europe for the Community!" After this she troubled him no further. In the same month Hawthorne sent two letters to Sophia Peabody, which seem to have been the last written her from Brook Farm. On July 9, of the next year, they were married.

Curtis once wrote in the Easy Chair that Hawthorne showed no marked affection for

Brook Farm, although Hawthorne himself has referred to his stay there as the one romantic episode of his life. The intimate nature of his note-books reveals the state of his feelings, although allowance is to be made for the spirit of banter and the half sincerities which are apt to pervade mere jottings and memoranda. If sympathy was wanting toward Transcendentalism itself, or its concrete expression through the Association, yet Hawthorne's genius worked out some interesting, if not especially profitable, results. In spite of frequent warnings and disclaimers regarding the book, in some contrary fashion the "Blithedale Romance" has come to be regarded as the epic of Brook Farm. An intelligent consideration of this story — a story of the second rank in Hawthorne's work — makes it clear that he was far more of a realist than is usually conceded. Harsh, for instance, as his interpretation of Margaret Fuller was, she doubtless appeared to him exactly as he described her. Seeing her unlovely attributes more clearly than he was able to see anything else, this realistic tendency, a sort of mental near-sightedness, impelled him to his ungracious task. There was a trend in favor of accurate rather than of fanciful and disguised use of literary material. Though the pen reluctantly comes to the writing of it, there was also in Hawthorne a fondness for discovering the forbidding aspects of a personality or a situation — a willingness to minimize.

Hawthorne was gentle by birth and training, and his occasional indelicacies are, for this reason, the less acceptable. Whenever he was able to free himself from circumstantiality and to rise on the wings of his imagination, he left beneath him these afflicting trammels. But he did not invariably escape into the empyrean, and the "Blithedale Romance" is one instance in which he hardly attempted a lofty flight. Having clearly in mind certain incidents and experiences at Brook Farm, some of which amused and irritated him, he did not avoid the impulse to tell these happenings pretty nearly as he found them, until, unsubstantial as the characters may or may not be, the daily life and doings, the scenery, the surroundings, and even trivial details are presented with a well-nigh faultless accuracy. Whoever chances to know the topography and history of Brook Farm, must of necessity follow the "Blithedale Romance" from the opening transcript of the author's arrival in the April storm, through real scenes and real events corresponding only too faithfully with the *mise-en-scène* and movement of the Brook Farm Association. It is no crime to have so thinly disguised actualities, only a fair and legitimate method of literary procedure. The characters are not easily traceable, but even in this respect Hawthorne did not free himself from the impressions once received and never to be obliterated from his sensitized nature. It matters little whether or not Zenobia is a blend of Miss Fuller and Mrs. Barlow; there certainly is more than an intimation of both. Arthur Sumner says that nobody at Brook Farm distantly resembled Zenobia; but a boy in his teens could not have gained impressions such as a woman like Hawthorne's heroine would have made upon an older man. Mrs. Kirby says that Zenobia was a friend of Miss Peabody, and died in Florence in the eighties. The same writer affirms that the original of Priscilla was a pretty, black-eyed girl who had been used as a clairvoyant in medical practice, but who, probably because she was a Roman Catholic, had ceased to develop her marked powers. In the strongest and most repellent character, Hollingsworth, Hawthorne may have incorporated something of the fierce, almost tiresome earnestness of Brownson or the pathetic zeal of Ripley. But here the fusion of the separate constituents has been complete, and a fresh character moulded, bearing only the true stamp of the artist's work. Minot Pratt is said, not without reason, to be the original of Silas Foster. These creations are Hawthorne's own, after all has been said. It would be unwise to conjecture how far a sense of his own insufficiency at the Farm may have affected his coloring of the picture. Curtis thought that Hawthorne's aloofness and want of effective support resembled the attitude of Charles Lamb toward life. " He had a subtle and pervasive humor, but no spirits," wrote the same friendly hand. A less generous critic might have said that Hawthorne expressed for his own uses the essential values of Brook Farm, and then speedily tired of it. Mrs. Kirby held that he was out of place, and " obtained the fruits of observation at second hand."

Hawthorne was not untrue to himself at Brook Farm, unless in going there at all he was capricious — his heart being involved in no affair of social regeneration. But even in his sombre genius there was some gladness, and a true romantic impulse may have drawn him thither, though he made no pretence of accepting the new gospel. The whole experience stands as a thing apart and unrelated to the rest of his life. Such complete detachment cannot be affirmed of any other of those who gave reputation to or borrowed it from Brook Farm.

John Orvis and John Allen

Brook Farmers have usually treated their early experience, not as a folly of youth, but in a partly tender, partly vague way which serves to veil, perhaps not intentionally, what is so hopelessly gone except in recollection. Self-respect would save these memories from cynicism or ridicule, but the bold declaration of a continuing faith and practice is rare; John Orvis, however, stands conspicuous for an abiding devotion to the principles of Association. His loyalty to the sentiment of justice was a legitimate inheritance from his parents, who were Hicksite Quakers, and although he ceased to be a member of the Society of Friends when he was still young, he never abandoned that conception of life into which he had been born and reared. His youth was spent on his father's beautiful farm in Ferrisburg, Vermont, where he laid the foundations for the superb health which in after years enabled him to lavish a boundless energy on great tasks. His early intellectual training, which he received principally at the hands of an Englishman named Wholley, was not comprehensive; he afterward became a student at Oberlin College, but never finished his course. He came to Boston while still a youth, and finding himself in the midst of the antislavery agitation, he lost no time in espousing this cause. Late in 1843 or early in 1844 he decided to share the fortunes of Brook Farm, and having chosen to become a member of the Farming Group, he worked with notable earnestness and good humor. John Cheever, whose wit was not fine enough, perhaps, to discriminate between positiveness of conviction and self-importance, used to call

Orvis "John Almighty," not, however, to Orvis's marked discomfiture.

When Fourierism was introduced, Orvis was called to the more important work of lecturing through the country in behalf of the general cause, and for the interest of Brook Farm in particular. An extract from one of his letters to the *Harbinger*, written during a tour in Vermont in February, 1846, illustrates the spirit in which he and his associate lecturer, John Allen, met hardships. "Our lectures were not successful there (Brattleboro) the first evening. The second evening they were quite satisfactory, both to ourselves and the audience, as far as we could judge. . . . I think we succeeded in giving a tolerably fair expression of the aims of Association. The next day we sent our trunks to Putney by stage and walked ourselves, it being only ten miles." The trunks were missing at Putney, and Orvis consumed a winter's day in tracing them to Walpole, Allen proceeding to Saxtonsville to keep an appointment that evening. On the following morning Orvis set out for the same place in a conveyance loaned by a friend. "This was more than kind," he says, "for it was the stormiest day of the winter, and we had to ride nine miles in the teeth of a fierce Northeaster, the roads filled with snow, and a perfectly unbroken track. But we had a noble steed, and a brave mountain driver who had trifled with storms from his boyhood. We got through in about two hours, really enjoying the ride." Allen had lectured to about fifty people the evening before, "after lighting his own fire, and borrowing lamps from the tavern to light the hall, and ringing the bell himself." The second evening was so stormy that no lecture was held. Just why midwinter should have been selected as a propitious season for visiting the villages of the Green Mountain state is not, on the surface, apparent; but, timely or not, the ardor of John Orvis and John Allen was not to be cooled by so trifling an obstacle as unseasonableness. Orvis was a particularly convincing speaker, for not only did he possess a clear, rich, and beautifully modulated voice, but his simple and earnest manner of presenting his subject carried great weight. He was not without humor, and the introduction to his review of Guénon's " Treatise on Milch Cows " is too pleasant not to be quoted: " Here is another new discovery under the sun — a veritable discovery, a French discovery. This last fact will, perhaps, seriously compromise its popularity in this country. Our good puritanic people will no doubt discover a tendency to *infidelity* or French *licentiousness* in it, and therefore reject it, as they do almost everything with which a Frenchman has to do." The discovery itself seems worth mentioning as one which has not yet revolution-

N

ized the dairy, viz. : that the quality and quantity of milk which any cow will give, and the length of time that she will continue to give it, can be accurately told by observing the hair, or "escutcheon," and dandruff on the posterior parts of the animal.

After the Phalanstery fire — a catastrophe which Orvis did not witness — his zeal redoubled for the sinking cause. Mrs. Ripley speaks of his return after lecturing, at this period, "rather worn down and disappointed, but with undying hope, faith, and devotion." So far as he was able he gained subscribers to the stock. With a few more members like Orvis, Pratt, and Mrs. Ripley, Brook Farm might have weathered all storms.

On December 24, 1846, John Orvis was married to John Dwight's sister, Marianne, who came to the Farm in the fall of 1843. During her early stay she taught Latin and drawing, and she always helped with some of the household work ; but later, a demand having arisen for her water-color sketches of the wild flowers of the district, she gave almost her entire time to supplying them. It was not an unusual thing for her to spend eight hours a day in her little studio at the Pilgrim House, autumn leaves supplying her with material for work when the flowers had passed by. Mrs. Orvis is still living.

After leaving Brook Farm Orvis took up, for

a time, insurance and the selling of sewing ma-
chines; but with his uncommon skill for organization, his ability as a lecturer, and his desire
for social reform, the career of a business man
did not sit easily on his soul.   In 1862 he
went to England to study the workings of co-
operation, investigating with especial care the
Rochdale plan.   His return in 1865 was the
beginning of a systematic effort to introduce co-
operative stores into this country; but although
the attempt yielded good results in some parts of
the West, it failed in the East, largely through
bad management.

The Patrons of Husbandry, a coöperative society made up of farmers, having attained large
proportions and a certain stability, a feeling
began to disseminate itself in favor of a similar
organization for the mechanical trades, and this
sentiment culminated in 1874, largely through
the efforts of William H. Earle, in the formation
of the Sovereigns of Industry — a secret order.
To the firm establishing of this order John Orvis brought his trained intelligence and his unabated strength as a lecturer and an organizer.
When the National Council of this association
appointed him as its national lecturer, it imposed
on him for two years grave responsibilities for
which it offered but slight remuneration.   But
Orvis was too much occupied with his endeavor
to transform a theory into a condition, to pay

attention to the monetary aspect of his labor; he believed that the principle of coöperation could be as effectively employed in the production as in the distribution of wealth; and to the task of elucidating this conviction he applied every resource of his mind, his tongue, and his pen.

His contributions to papers and magazines were numerous and telling; in addition to his other duties he edited the *Sovereigns of Industry Bulletin*. Though the Order grew very rapidly, there was so great a delay in adopting the Rochdale system that many of the stores, which were to buy at wholesale and sell at cost, were undersold by competitors and forced out of business; and in 1879, or thereabouts, the project was abandoned.

In a proper sense he was a labor agitator; he had the qualities which characterize the best English protagonists in this cause, in that he was not blatant or self-seeking. He defended the trades-unions, and was himself a member of the Knights of Labor, although he deprecated many of the methods to which these bodies resorted. Nationalism, also, had its charm for him as a possible avenue of escape from existing inequalities.

It was a part of Orvis's social creed that to Brook Farm were traceable many of the movements which for the past fifty years in America have looked toward the improvement of indus-

trial conditions; and although his disappointment grew as one star of hope after another
rose and set, he was no more a sceptic in regard
to social possibilities when he died, in April,
1897, than he had been as a Brook Farmer.
He was of too sturdy a fibre, and his beliefs
were too fundamental, for him to abandon faith
in anything but a concrete experiment, which
had actually been tried and failed. With all
his strength, his tastes were delicate; music,
pictures, rural beauty, children, gave him keen
delight; and his exuberant health made anything but cheerfulness and buoyancy an impossibility. Always a student and a reader, he
was, despite his moderate early acquirements,
an exceedingly well informed man; and the
natural generosity of his mind, which was fully
matched by the generosity of his heart, developed under self-cultivation into a rare toleration
which much enhanced the value and prominence
of his work and influence.

The Rev. John Allen was a Universalist who
had the good sense to leave a ministry which
had forgotten the injunction to preach the gospel to every creature. His reason was a simple
one : he disbelieved in slavery, and was willing
to say so, even from the pulpit. His church
disbelieved in slavery too, but the subject was
annoying. Mr. Allen was moderate indeed and
conciliatory; he consented to levy on the Amer-

ican right of free speech, and on his duty as he saw it, only once a year. At first he pleaded valiantly for indulgence in this constitutional privilege once in three months, then once in six months. This was denied; and when the congregation refused him one day annually in which to speak his mind, he left a profession and became a man. The experience was a common one in those days; but Allen did not place the alternative of livelihood ahead of obvious duty. He went to Brook Farm, which welcomed any brave man, though it professed no especial love for abolitionism. Allen had the delicacy not to try to make his new home a College of the Propaganda, but put his skill at preaching to ready use. Orvis and he, during the two years which followed the adoption of the Brisbanized Fourierism, lectured on Association and especially on Brook Farm. Both were good organizers and practical men. Allen called a meeting of delegates, held at Lowell in 1844, and presided over by Ryckman; and out of this call came the New England Workingmen's Association, which sought specifically to secure by legislation a ten-hour working day.

John Allen did not sufficiently believe in vaccination to protect, in the accepted manner, his only and motherless child from the danger of smallpox. The boy was sometimes left with his aunt, Mrs. Leach, while his father was away on lecture tours, and in September, 1845, the scourge came back with him from Boston. The Leaches had withdrawn from Brook Farm in 1843 to open a Grahamite hotel, and Mrs. Leach, who was a stout abolitionist, relieved the monotony of a vegetarian life by harboring runaway slaves. Her husband, George C. Leach, was as silent as his wife was voluble, and he is said to have found peace in the Roman Catholic Church. Mrs. Leach was a deadly foe to the " fix-ups " in which the young girls at the Farm sometimes indulged, although these were of the simplest description. Her little nephew's misfortune resulted from his association with a man servant who had been suffering from a cold, attended with an eruption, the nature of which was discovered soon after the child's return to Brook Farm. The little fellow was at once removed from the Hive, but too late to prevent an epidemic of moderate proportions. Over thirty cases of smallpox appeared; the Cottage was turned into a hospital, and the wise method of isolation put into practice until the patients grew too numerous. There was no fatal case, only a few cases were serious, and, admirable to tell, there was no panic. It was a severe test of the social and mental strength of the Associates that women and men moved calmly and easily about, keeping the work going, and nursing as best they could. Allen's fanatical carelessness brought about a valuable experience, and for a time drove away the visitors. The son grew to manhood, enlisted in the Civil War, and was wounded, as it proved, mortally, at Vicksburg. The second wife of John Allen was Ellen Lazarus, whose father was at Brook Farm. The Allens went West, but the wife, unable to contend against the severities of the change, soon died.

Minot Pratt   Perhaps Mr. Ripley's most trusted adviser in matters relating to the practical management of the farm was Minot Pratt, who, during the months of conference and preparation, had given Ripley's scheme his sympathy and support. Mrs. Pratt and her three children were among the pioneers at the Farm, but Mr. Pratt did not arrive until two or three months later. He was a printer, and had held for some time the position of foreman in the *Christian Register* office; many details, therefore, had to be arranged before he could permanently abandon his work there.

Pratt was about thirty-six years old when he went to Brook Farm, where he was soon recognized as an important and beloved factor in the life. He became head farmer at the end of the first season. Although Pratt had had no experience in farm work, he took to it as a man who had always believed that he was not meant to be a printer; and he rapidly acquired a sound working knowledge of practical agriculture which, it has been thought, would have averted financial disaster had it been supplemented by an equivalent wisdom on the part of even a few of his fellow workers. He became a trustee of the Association in April, 1843, taking the place left vacant by the withdrawal of Ichabod Morton, and filling it with distinction so long as he stayed at the Farm. Certain qualities of his character, as they disclosed themselves, revealed his peculiar worthiness for the trust reposed in him. Honesty and courage of the most unflinching variety, sagacity of judgment, and fineness of temper — these, attended with a voice and manner of exceeding gentleness, caused the balance of feeling toward him on the part of his fellows to show an almost perfect adjustment between love and confidence.

His fondness for all forms of life was very genuine, and was manifested with the same quiet force which he showed in handling practical or moral problems. His passion was botany; but it was not a mere scientific passion, since a feeling for beauty was one of its largest ingredients. It sometimes gave him joy to rescue the wild flowers and rose-bushes which were uprooted by the morning's ploughing, and carefully replant them along the edge of the town road as a future solace to the passer-by. Although he

must be classed with the inarticulate brother-
hood, he seems none the less to have had some
claim to the qualities and temperament of a
poet in his fine appreciations.

The Pratt family lived at the Hive during
their four years of residence on the Farm, and
their youngest child, Theodore Parker Pratt,
was the first child born there. Mrs. Pratt, whose
belief in the associative life was fully as deep
as her husband's, lived up to her faith as honestly and bravely as he, and she and her children were very happy in the community. But
both Mr. and Mrs. Pratt foresaw, rather early,
the termination of the Phalanx, and felt that
they ought not to wait until that event left them
stranded before seeking some other means of
providing a livelihood for their family. Though
they both approved the grafting of Fourieristic
variations upon the old life, it is doubtful whether
they gave a very cordial assent to some of the con-
comitant changes; and in April, 1845, they reluctantly left West Roxbury to take possession of
a farm which they had hired at Concord. Sad-
dened as were Ripley and the others at this
loss, they recognized the justice of Pratt's arguments that his children were still too young
to add anything to the productiveness of the
Association and were, therefore, to that extent,
a burden upon it; and that the farm was in a
condition to be deprived of his services without

serious embarrassment. If he decided to say nothing of his deeper reasons, it is characteristic that in his letter of farewell he could only express a hope — not a belief — that "this attempt to live out the great and holy idea of association for brotherly coöperation" might meet with final success.

Mr. Pratt later bought the Concord farm and spent there the remainder of his life, continuing in the intervals of agricultural toil his botanical studies, and writing his "Flora of Concord," the manuscript of which is held by the Concord Library. He has been described as one of the "most conspicuously attractive inhabitants" of the Hive — large and of fine physique, with strong features, and a modest but dignified mien. He died on March 29, 1878, his wife surviving him until May, 1891, when she died somewhat past eighty, the last of the signers of the original agreement.

George Partridge Bradford, who figures as the Dominie in Mrs. Kirby's *Old and New* papers, was another of the Brook Farm clergymen who had felt the inadequacy of the pulpit as a medium of social service. Mere formality and conventionalism would not sit easily on the son of so sturdy a revolutionary soldier as Captain Gamaliel Bradford, once of Duxbury. The latter, whose wife was Elizabeth Hickling, had several children, of whom

George Partridge Bradford

George was the youngest; he was born on February 16, 1807. When he was ten years old his mother died, and he became the special charge of his sister Sarah, who, in 1818, married the Rev. Samuel Ripley, of Waltham. Mrs. Ripley helped her husband to prepare young men for college. She was a genuine Transcendentalist, and in recognition of the fact Emerson gave her one of the three copies of "Sartor Resartus" which Carlyle sent to America. Of the remaining two copies, Emerson kept one himself and gave the other to Hedge. Mrs. Dall, in her comprehensive lecture on "Transcendentalism in New England," does not hesitate to say that the picture of Parson Allen's home, as drawn by Saxe Holm in "My Tourmaline," is a tribute to Mr. and Mrs. Samuel Ripley.

The guidance and companionship of this gifted woman were potent formative influences on a mind with strong natural prepossessions toward philosophic thought. Bradford was of the class of 1825 at Harvard, and was graduated three years later from the Divinity School, where he would gladly have been retained as an instructor if he had felt willing to stay; for even at that time his ability as a teacher was evidently suspected if not well known. Although he delivered an occasional sermon, he never took a regular parish, partly for causes already alluded to, and partly because he recognized certain limitations of temperament in himself. Perhaps, too, the straightforward comment of Dr. Andrews Norton may have acted not as a stimulating douche, but as an extinguishing wet blanket: " Your discourse, Mr. Bradford, is marked by the absence of every qualification which a good sermon ought to have; " and the suggestion, despite the differing points of view of the two men, was timely enough to insure acceptance by the fair-minded Bradford.

Teaching soon commended itself to him as the work in which his tastes and training could best be utilized, and his first class was gathered in Plymouth, where he received such pupils — mostly girls — as were able by inclination or by opportunity to draw upon the wide resources of his scholarship. One marked peculiarity of his mind, which reflected itself in his conduct, was an inability to confine himself for any length of time within prescribed limits. After a year or two of work in one place he would begin to fancy that the quality of his teaching was falling off a little, or that, for some other reason, it would be better to abandon the present undertaking and start afresh. This almost morbid self-distrust, which gradually lessened as he grew older, was a singular weakness in so discriminating an intellect, but it nevertheless produced a peculiarly lovable character. Curtis thinks

that his restlessness was not of nervous origin, but was only an expression of "fulness
of life and sympathy." Mrs. Ripley once said
of Bradford that he would not be happy in
heaven unless he could see his way out.

It was nothing but what might have been
expected, then, that Bradford should join that
"company of teachers" at Brook Farm, at the
very outset, for they were men with whose previous spiritual strivings he had had much in common, and for whose purpose he felt the sincerest
friendliness. He naturally fell into place in the
school, and his gentle and kindly enthusiasm
stimulated the general growth in mental health.
Mrs. Kirby says that he was "one of those born
at thirty-four, who would never get any older,"
and the friends of his later life have always
been ready to substantiate this assertion. The
slight tempering of his wit and vivacity by
his occasional gentle melancholy resulted in the
sort of humor which has happily been called
quaint. On one occasion some of the Brook
Farm maidens took their lunch to Parker's
church, in order to avoid the long walk between
the services, and they insisted on having their
impromptu picnic in the pulpit, as a protest
against the superstition that there was anything
sacred about that particular piece of wood. The
Dominie, who had accompanied the party to
church, shook his head reproachfully, and said

that "he wished to retain the superstition about the wood, since he had once occupied the pulpit himself."

That Bradford's service to the Association was not wholly intellectual, is shown by a sentence in a letter written to Hawthorne by his sister while he was still at the Farm. "Mr. George Bradford," she writes, italicizing as only a sister can, "one of your *brethren*, has paid a visit in Lowell, where I understand his *hands* excited great astonishment." Bradford came honestly by these callous hands, for he worked in the hay field, milked cows, dug peat, and "pounded" clothes in a barrel—a task which must be performed to be properly appreciated. Bradford was a fine botanist and an expert in market-gardening, his special delight being, when he went to see Emerson, to give advice if not actual help about the vegetables and to trim the trees; and it is clear that the sage did not consider this expert knowledge the least admirable of his friend's accomplishments.

Although Bradford spoke with some approval at first of Fourier, he did not stay to help reconstruct the community. He believed Fourier to have had "a rare and original mind"; but he was also aware that "our nobler part protests at much which a genuine descendant of the old Puritans must always find it hard to swallow." It is recounted of him that he came down stairs

at the Hive one morning, clad in a long over-
coat, and carrying an umbrella and a package
wrapped up in a blue silk handkerchief. He
had before intimated that he could not cordially
approve the Association's attitude toward the
outside world, and that the "idea" did not seem
quite so acceptable to him as he had hoped;
and he now announced his plan of migrating
to Plymouth, where he meant to start, with his
friend Marston Watson, a little market-garden
of his own. Before leaving, however, he asked
one or two of the young women who had always
shown a feeling of affectionate admiration for
him to hear a portentous confession which he
felt impelled to make, although he realized that
in so doing he must forfeit their regard forever.
The lack of seriousness with which this prelude
was received disturbed the gentle Dominie more
than his sense of guilt; but trusting to the horrors
of the revelation itself to make a proper impression, he declared boldly that there had been times
when he would not have lifted a finger to save
Charles Dana's life, had he been in immediate
danger of losing it, so jealous was he (Bradford)
at Dana's success in luring into his German class
the very girls whom Bradford himself longed to
instruct in that language.

The kindly scholar thus took his leave and
worked among his own vegetables. Watson
and he sold them in person to Plymouth house-

keepers and received the handsome tribute that for once here were market-gardeners who knew their place, since they always brought their goods to the back door. Bradford eventually resumed his chosen profession, carrying it on in various places, and occasionally exchanging its joys for those of travel. Seven trips to Europe helped to prevent his falling into the mere routine of teaching, although there is little likelihood that he would ever have succumbed to a weakness against which constitutional prejudice protected him. His literary achievement was slight for a man of his scholarship and tastes; he edited, however, some admirable selections from Fénelon, and finished the luminous and comprehensive chapter on " Philosophic Thought in Boston" which Ripley had sketched for the fourth volume of Winsor's "Memorial History." His literary judgment was sound and as independent as his politics, in which he gave allegiance to ideas rather than to parties or men. He was devoutly though not gloomily religious; yet here, also, he was bound by no tenets. Although in later life he became deaf, his intellectual vigor did not wane, and he never grew indifferent to the interests of his youth. Mr. Bradford did not marry, but he had the confidence and friendship of many noble women, some of whom were glad to ascribe to his instruction their love for many good things.

o

When he died suddenly on January 26, 1890, those who had known him long realized that, little as there was to chronicle in his uneventful career, his sweetness and refinement, always discernible in his face, had contributed an imperishable fragrance to their lives.

An instance of Bradford's hopeless honesty is told by President Walker, to whom he applied for the position of Librarian at Harvard College. Instead of unfolding his qualifications, Bradford elaborately gave every possible reason why he should not have the place, much to the good President's astonishment.

Warren Burton, who joined the organizing party in the spring of 1841, was a native of Wilton, New Hampshire, where he was born in 1800. There must be fundamental soundness in a nature on which such corroding ills as Burton suffered when a child leave no scar. The faith of many a youth has been permanently darkened by less severe religious perturbations than those through which he passed, in his attempts to accept the theology of the day and yet follow the leadings of his own warm affections. His first troubles came at the age of four, from what he read and from the conversations which he heard; but he told himself that when he grew old enough to go to church, seeming contradictions would be explained and his doubts would vanish. Great, then, was his dismay to find that

"his understanding in divine things was still further darkened at the house of worship," and that
the problem must be wrestled with alone. As
his mind unfolded under the influence of study,
general reading, and observation, and he came to
understand the function of a figure of speech,
much of the terror of the earlier days faded;
the multiplication of interests made it easy not
to focus his thoughts on the theological puzzle.
At fifteen the "melancholy superstition" had
passed and he had "escaped a conversion and a
zeal without knowledge." For some time the
inevitable reaction set in; religion became a
wholly neglected subject, until his later study of
the Bible and his profound love of nature established a normal readjustment between his moral
and spiritual life. Having put behind him a
boyhood tortured not only with religious doubts,
but with acute dyspepsia, — a youth rendered
peculiarly lonely through the early loss of his
mother, and through the fact that he was an
only child, — Burton entered college a mature,
overthoughtful young man, though a very child
in simplicity. He was almost wholly self-pre-
pared for academic work, the district school and
the occasional help of the parish minister having
been his only sources of instruction.

A member of the class of 1821 at Harvard
he received his second degree in 1825, and was
graduated from the Divinity School in 1826.

His first parish was that of the Third (Unitarian) Congregational Church at East Cambridge, which he took in March, 1828, and where he remained until June, 1829. At the close of his service there he declined, for a time, to accept another appointment, preferring to use the opportunity afforded him as a "minister at large" to carry out certain educational projects to which he felt committed. Accordingly, not until September, 1833, do we find him again a settled minister; but at that time he became the pastor of a church in South Hingham which he served until 1835, when he was called to take charge of the Second Religious Society in Waltham. In the year following his removal to Waltham, his beloved wife, Sarah Flint, whom he had married in 1828, died. This woman, whose character was as rare as her beauty, had been his friend and companion from boyhood, and her loss so told upon him that he abandoned his work in April, 1837, and again threw himself into the cause of popular education. The great responsibility devolving on home influences in the matter of education and culture was his special theme, and his stay at Brook Farm only strengthened his belief in the importance of his mission.

Little is recorded of his community life beyond the fact that he came in the spring of 1841 and was gone in the spring of 1844; but if anything may be inferred from his later fervor and buoyancy under discouraging conditions, it is that his character must at all times have endeared him to his fellows, and that he returned to the world fortified and resolute.

From August, 1844, until October, 1848, he was a minister at large in Boston, and during 1849–1850 he occupied a like position in Worcester, acting also in 1849 as chaplain of the Worcester prison. From that time until his death lecturing and writing absorbed him, although he found time to perform the duties incumbent upon the chaplain of the State Senate in 1852, of the House in 1850, and again in 1860, and of the State Constitutional Convention in 1853. As is the way with ministers at large, he was very poor, yet he seems never to have been disturbed by so irrelevant a fact. If he could deliver a course of lectures on his favorite topic to large and interested audiences, he cared little whether there were pecuniary returns. In addition to his poverty, his later years of work were seriously hampered by ill health; still these twin harpies produced no sensible modification of purpose and no diminution of courage. His "Helps to Education" was a worthy contribution to this overconsidered question, and his "District School as it Was" is the joint production of wisdom and humor. Burton's mother is thought to be the original of the teacher — Mary Smith — of this book. "Scenery Shower" is a little book of quite another type, for it sets forth the moral worthiness of nature as a subject for observation and study. "Scenery Showing" is the title of a later edition, to avoid an obvious ambiguity in the first title.

Burton became an eager disciple of Swedenborg, whose doctrines had aroused more or less interest at Brook Farm, and showed, according to the *Dial*, marked affinity with those of Fourier; but it is said that he held these doctrines in no narrow sense. He also took a deep interest in phrenology. His manner was full of cordiality, and the eagerness and vitality of youth persisted in his talk long after his physical frame had yielded to disease and pain. In September, 1845, he had married Mary Merritt of Salem, who, in his last illness, cared for him with tireless affection. His two children had both died when comparatively young, and Burton himself died in Salem in 1866.

The perplexities and pleasures of the community were matters of equal indifference to Charles Newcomb, whose aloofness from the general life marks him as a person for special consideration. He came from Providence, where he had been graduated from Brown University in 1837, at the age of seventeen. He had, as a youth, looked forward to the ministry as his profession, "but soon found it impossible to be a sectarian." He attached

Charles King Newcomb

himself to the Farm in the early days as a "full boarder" — not because he felt at that time any irresistible passion for the uplifting of mankind, but because he saw that the seclusion and the simplicity of the life would put no barrier in the way of loafing and inviting his soul. Charles Newcomb thought a good deal about the soul. He was deeply versed in the literature of mysticism, which he dearly loved, and according to Emerson "he hated intellect with the ferocity of a Swedenborg." Emerson was convinced that Newcomb's remarkable subtlety of mind amounted to genius, and he assured Margaret Fuller that certain sentences in "Dolon," Newcomb's sole contribution, apparently, to the *Dial* were "worth the printing of the *Dial* that they may go forth." One sentence from this curious paper indicates, if not genius, its next of kin : " A child will act from the fulness of its affections and feelings as if from consciousness, but these are the spirit which thus affect him, and he acts from them as facts which buoy him up and float him, not as sentiment which is need of the fact, and makes him a seeker, as men, who away from their home, or outwardly related to their sphere, feel that which develops in them sentiment and aspiration, but does not put them in the natural position of the sentiment, and the sentiment thus acts, out of its place, from depths which the surface in its hurried

action, is as if dissevered from." Grammar, next
to intellect, was his dearest foe.

Newcomb was a sentimental devotee of un-
attached Catholicism, fascinated by its "psalms
and anthems and dramatic rites," but scornful
of its other claims. In his room at the Eyrie
were pictures of such of the Church's canonized
ones as possessed the qualities which he admired.
He was fond of lending the works of St. Augus-
tine and similar books to his neighbors, and
was given to reciting the litany in the middle
of the night. When he first heard of Fanny
Ellsler's arrival in Boston, he denounced her
as a "vile creature"; but, having seen her, he
placed her portrait between that of Loyola and
Xavier. If, on a Sunday morning in winter, as
he skated along the river, this feverish young
man should happen to detect a church spire at no
great distance from the shore, it would give him
the profoundest satisfaction to remove his skates,
seek out the church, enter it, skates in hand,
kneel a moment at the altar, and return briskly
to his sport.

Communion with himself and Nature (the
spelling of which without a capital would have
seemed blasphemous to him) was the chosen oc-
cupation of his life; and if, when he felt the need
of other companionship, he sought the society of
children oftener than that of his contemporaries,
it was because children were nearer to Nature

and Life than were men, — whose "relations to Nature are closed by their coming between the realities of soul and Nature," — whatever that may mean. His vagaries engendered amusement and sometimes surprise even in this colony where idiosyncrasies were generously condoned. He was, as a matter of course, exceedingly sensitive to "atmosphere," and is said by Mrs. Kirby, to whose readers he is known as Erasmus, to have changed his seat at table because he resented the "profound exactions" made by the eyes of his unconscious feminine vis-à-vis.

There was an all-around lack of vigor in the youth. Slight in body, uncertain in carriage, with eyes of a peculiar expression which betrayed his introspective habits, a prominent nose and long, dark, rather unkempt hair, he carried an air of mystery about him that allured rather than repelled. He alone, of the dwellers in this oasis, held up contemplation as a cult.

Although he failed, for some reason, to make his real ability felt, there is no doubt that he was gifted to an unusual degree. After leaving West Roxbury he returned to Providence and, in 1862, served for three months in the Tenth Rhode Island Volunteer Infantry. In 1870 he went to Europe for a permanent residence, living mostly in London and Paris. On one occasion he spent some time in Rome with his Brook

Farm friend, George Bradford. It is understood that Mr. Newcomb did a large amount of literary work, but so far as is known he did not publish it. He died suddenly in Paris in 1894.

CHAPTER V

THE VISITORS

THE visitors were many and welcome to the simple hospitalities of board and even of bed, until their numbers grew from a few friends, who would run out to see how this Republic of lovable fools was faring, to a steadily increasing host of all kinds and conditions of reformers, and followers of reform, curiosity seekers, hostile critics, the partly mad, and the wholly mad. There was at the Hive a Visitors' Book, now lost, which is said to have contained four thousand entries made in a single year.

In spite of this heavy burden of hospitality laid so unreasonably on the small community, it was borne with distinguished courtesy, although many of the visitors came uninvited and evidently felt that they had much to receive, but little to return. When the slender resources could no longer stand this undue strain, a modest fee for each meal was asked, and paid, though sometimes with reluctance. There was, no doubt, something of policy in this urbanity toward the guests. The Brook Farmers were willing that

their light should shine before men to the end
that outsiders might be moved to the right way
of thinking, and perhaps of living. The fee may
have acted as a deterrent; but when curiosity
was, in a measure, gratified and the momentary
fascination past, the mass of visitors dwindled
away, normal conditions reasserted themselves,
and only true friends or relatives of the Associates and the inevitable camp followers of reform
made their calls.

It was no wonder that many should be drawn
to this little Mecca of the Newness. There was
news abroad of the boldness of the project,
the beauty of the place, and the odd but delightful character of the inmates. And so it
fell out that there was much running to West
Roxbury to learn how the chosen people were
prospering. The excitements of Boston have
ever been few; and to see the regeneration of
mankind going on under your own nose and
eyes, with little or nothing to pay, proved an ex-
hilarating and instructive experience. Notwithstanding the trouble to which the members were
now and then put to provide accommodation of
every sort, these visitors proved an important
element in the history of Brook Farm, adding to its renown and somewhat to its charm.
Some came from long distances, and some were
people of real distinction. Among artists, were
Story, Cranch, Sartain, Ordway, and Champ-

ney, naturally drawn to the beauty of the scene and the romantic features attending it. Publicists, editors, men of affairs, came from New York and even from distant parts of the country and from abroad. Robert Owen once made a visit and was well received, though his views little accorded with those of Brook Farm. But the clergy, and in particular the Unitarian clergy, were most numerous among those whose names were of some note. A Unitarian, himself a religious radical, could not well think of his Transcendental friends as heretic, although they certainly were schismatic. Good will, a fine toleration, and a genuine interest in the experiment brought the clergy to West Roxbury sure of a cordial greeting. One good champion of orthodoxy, Father Taylor, was an occasional guest. The neighbors must not be forgotten, for it was their clear privilege to "run in" on the community at any time. Of these good friends, George R. Russell, Francis G. Shaw, and Theodore Parker, and their respective families, were the most conspicuous and most devoted. Each of these men showed his friendliness toward the enterprise by taking mortgages on the estate. The records of the Norfolk Registry of Deeds show that Russell and Shaw used to transfer the mortgages which they held from one to the other, as if for the sake of variety. Neighborliness, a helpful spirit, and a willingness to hold securities represented the extent of their faith in the theories of Mr. Ripley and his companions. There is little need to enumerate the celebrities, both men and women, who paid their respects to Brook Farm. They came, were amused or edified for the while, and then went their way. Some may have gone to scoff, but few indeed remained to pray.

A few choice visitors have always been so closely identified with the fame of Brook Farm that their connection with it has come to be an integral part of its history. Chief among them were Margaret Fuller, Emerson, William Henry Channing, Alcott, Charles Lane, Cranch, Brownson, Horace Greeley, Albert Brisbane, and Elizabeth Peabody. There also came Hedge, Higginson, and Lowell; these, however, came but seldom, and had no close identification with the life of the Associates. With the distinguished group first mentioned Brook Farm had a real affinity. The relations may have been closer in some cases than in others, but in each case they were important enough to demand a special consideration.

Notwithstanding the greeting which was extended to the majority of those who came to see Brook Farm, — and they often came, it must be admitted, in the same spirit in which they would have inspected a gypsy encampment, — it should not be forgotten that the Brook Farmers

professed to hold "civilisées," as they liked to
call the worldlings, in much contempt. This
was in part a playful conception; but a pitying
sentiment, such as Christian entertained for
the benighted City of Destruction, was natural
to these determined young separatists. Their
deeper regard was kept for the few who were
representative of the larger phases of Transcendentalism and Fourierism, and who were glad
from time to time to cheer their allies by their
presence and stimulating words. Of the relations
of these friends to Brook Farm it is fitting to
speak somewhat in detail. Horace Greeley, one
of the most conspicuous of this group, should
properly be mentioned later in these pages in
connection with Albert Brisbane and the Fourierist movement.

Although Margaret Fuller's connection **Margaret**
with Brook Farm was slight, no general ac- **Fuller**
count of the community fails to lay some empha-
sis on her relation to it and her attitude toward
it. Her position within the circle which had at
heart the success of this movement is indicated
by the fact that she is always associated with
them even in a matter with which she did not
deeply concern herself. Just why she looked
doubtfully on the effort is to be accounted
for in several ways, all of which necessitate a
somewhat scrutinizing glance at her earlier life;
for, at this time, she was over thirty, and she

had thought and felt, and therefore suffered, more than most men and women of that age.

On May 23, 1810, Margaret Fuller was born, the daughter of Timothy Fuller and Margaret Crane. Subsequent to this event the mother seems to have played an inconspicuous part in the life of the child, whose early education and training were wholly taken in charge by her father. Timothy Fuller, according to his daughter, had received from his father that kind of sound worldly advice which the Puritan clergyman's conscience has often permitted him to give — the admonition that he must make sure of two things: a position of professional distinction, and a sufficient income to maintain a family. These are, to be sure, only two phases of that ideal of success which has never ceased to be dear to both the church and the world. Starting with this, in a more or less modified form, as an inheritance, and left wholly to the care of the parent from whom it came, Margaret Fuller's chances of developing into a wholesome or noble maturity seemed slight indeed. The educational methods of the period were severe, and they were practised on her by her father with systematic, though unintentional, cruelty. Evening recitations, a good deal broken into at times, but never pretermitted on that account, produced the inevitable results attendant upon an overstimulated brain — nightmares, somnambulism, nervous exhaustion, and morbidness. Perhaps the child's salvation came from an inward rebellion, seemingly her only natural and healthy emotion. Nothing shows Mr. Fuller's limitations more distinctly than his complacent pride in his wholly unnatural daughter. She was regarded only in her relation to his system, and she undoubtedly gave clear proof that a naturally well endowed human being can, by injudicious forcing, develop into an intellectual prodigy. That she was an isolated, unhappy girl did not occur to him until irreparable damage had been inflicted on her body and mind. She is said by some one to have been an imaginative child, but this is improbable; for an imaginative nature could hardly have survived such an intellectual ordeal as she underwent between the ages of six and thirteen. In any case, no signs of such a faculty appear in her later literary work.

Two years at the school of the Misses Prescott in Groton did something toward counteracting her overdeveloped arrogance and self-esteem; for there she was treated, at a critical moment, like any ordinary personality, and the experience sank deep. The few who knew her well at that time did not doubt that there was sympathy, and even humility, lurking somewhere under the crust of sarcasm and hauteur which

P

was evident to all the world; but with the latter,
admiration for her attainments and her wit was
predominant. The harsher qualities of her youth
are thus insisted upon, because, in the writer's
opinion, Margaret Fuller's glory is that, one by
one, she exorcised these demons and substituted
for them a noble spirit of self-sacrifice and love.
We may "feel disposed," with George Eliot, "to
extend to her whole career the admiration and
sympathy inspired by the closing scenes," but
we should only show ourselves unjust toward
her highest accomplishment by so doing. Sincerity characterized her to the last, and her sense
of superiority, equally dominant in the beginning, dwindled under the gradual restraint imposed by her widening sympathies and interests.

Her activities seem to form themselves into
three distinct groups: those of preparation for
her work in New York on the *Tribune*, covering
the years of her teaching, her Conversations, and
her labors on the *Dial* (1837–1844); her achievements as critic on Greeley's newspaper (1844–
1846); and her life in Italy (1847–1850).

As a member of the Transcendental Club,
and as a close friend of the Ripleys, she had
taken part in the discussions which led to the
establishment of Brook Farm; but until within
a very short time of the taking of the final step
she did not believe that the project would be attempted. Toward the last of December, 1840,

she wrote: "I fancy the best use of the plan, as projected thus far, will prove the good talks it has caused here upon principles;" and on March 29, 1841, on the eve of the hegira, she said: "I do not know what their scheme will ripen to; at present it does not deeply engage my hopes. It is thus far only a little better way than others."

The spirit of toleration was of slow growth in Margaret Fuller, and at this time it had attained only respectable proportions. Her position is generally stated in an unpublished letter to Mrs. Chapman, dated December 26, 1840: "Very probably to one whose heart is so engaged as yours in particular measures, this indifference will seem incredible or even culpable. But, if indifferent, I have not been intolerant; I have wronged none of you by a hasty judgment or careless words, and, where I have not investigated a case so as to be sure of my own opinion, have, at least, never chimed in with the popular hue and cry. I have always wished that efforts originating in a generous sympathy or a sense of neglect should have fair play, [and] have had firm faith that they must, in some way, produce eventual good." The toleration of indifference is not an uncommon attribute; it is the toleration which is exercised in the face of one's own strong feelings of opposition that really counts. At the same time, it is not fair to lose sight of the fact that in the seven or eight years which preceded the making of this statement — years in which Miss Fuller had been obliged to renounce many of her own pleasures and ambitions in order to provide comfort for her mother, and education for her brothers and sisters — she had become far less self-centred and less disposed to bow before the god of intellect.

At Brook Farm, as in other places, there were differences of opinion regarding her greatness. Mrs. Kirby gave up her room at the Eyrie sometimes when Miss Fuller came, first burning pastilles as an appreciative preparation, and taking great pleasure in serving coffee every morning to the favored guest in her room, out of the only decorated china cup belonging to the estate. Miss Russell, on the other hand, seems not to have given an unqualified admiration to this visitor, of whom she says: "When listening to her wonderful conversations, which, by the way, were limited to one person — herself — and straining my mind to comprehend her meaning, I must own I have sometimes wished her English was rather plainer." Another woman is quoted as saying that she would like to have Margaret Fuller for a spiritual adviser. Margaret Fuller's own early impressions of the community are too familiar to need repetition here. It is true that she spoke freely of her own faults, but it has never been made clear that the criticism of others found ready acceptance with her;

and it is certain that she recognized her own virtues as generously as she did her shortcomings. She was still too much of an egotist and too little of a humorist to treat lightly any failure to take her at her own estimate. Humor, indeed, in its highest development, she did not have; otherwise she would have been too conscious of some of her own absurdities to indulge them. It was no secret among her friends that she sought Brook Farm primarily for solitude, and it is likely that her wish to be let alone was generally respected, and that she was left very much to herself, during the day at least, in accordance with the feeling expressed by Mrs. Kirby: "My great reverence for a person at once so remarkable, and so in need of rest and leisure, made me keep at a very careful distance." The pine woods so refreshed and soothed her that she retreated to them whenever the season permitted. It was her custom to spend New Year's Eve with the "fledglings of Community," and the deepening of her interest in their purpose, if not in their practice, is very apparent between 1841 and the New Year's Eve of 1844, when she recorded the strong feeling aroused in her by a recent Fourier convention and by a talk with Mrs. Ripley.

Miss Fuller's desire for a less hampered life having become possible through the completion of the education of her brothers, she accepted, with much satisfaction, an offer from Horace Greeley to become a permanent member of his staff. Her work on the *Dial* had first called his attention to her ability; but it was at the suggestion of Mrs. Greeley, who had come to know Miss Fuller well in the course of several visits to Boston, that he decided to put forward this opportunity to strengthen her own reputation and that of the *Tribune*.

It is easy to accept Miss Fuller's announcement, fortified by the assertions of her friends, that she talked better than she wrote. The "excess of reflective consciousness" which Charles Dana discerned in her "Papers on Literature and Art" was much less apparent in her talk, when she felt the stimulating friction of other minds and forgot herself. She did not particularly like literary work, because it forced her to a recognition of her own limitations; but realizing it as the only medium through which to reach large numbers of people, she readily determined to subject herself to its discipline. Greeley's early disappointment in her he explains as follows: "While I never met another woman who conversed more freely and lucidly, the attempt to commit her thoughts to paper seemed to induce a singular embarrassment and hesitation. She could write only when in the vein; and this needed often to be waited for through several days, while the occasion some-

times required an immediate utterance." The
long strain which she had undergone had doubtless produced a certain degree of exhaustion
which was in part responsible for this; and it
is also probable that the thought of the effect
which her writing might produce on the public
acted as a restraint on her. Mr. Greeley has
added a fine appreciation of the widespread
good accomplished by the unfaltering truthful-
ness of her work, however little this quality
may have added to her popularity. In their
first acquaintance Mr. Greeley and Miss Fuller
found themselves in imperfect accord on sundry
questions. He resented the exactions of defer-
ence made by a woman who was battling for
sex-equality; and she caustically rejected his
intimation that she would not have so many
headaches if she drank less tea and coffee.
These superficial disagreements, however, wore
away, and each came to make a just and sound
estimate of the other's excellences. Her sympathies broadened daily; and the result of her
contact with all sorts and conditions of men and
women was that she became a more and more
pronounced champion of the weak and neglected.

The residence in New York covered less than
two years, for it was in August, 1846, that she
went to Europe for her great and overwhelming
experience. The friends, the triumphs, and the

failures of her first year there must be ignored
for the sake of a passing glance at the spirit
which her Italian life called forth.   Secretly
married in the winter of 1847 to the young Mar-
chese d'Ossoli, who had become, partly, at least,
through her influence, one of the intrepid followers of Mazzini, she gave the fearless intensity of her best self to the Republican party.
With the birth of her son in September, 1848,
she cast aside the shackles which heredity had
imposed but which a continuous chain of circumstances had been steadily weakening; and in
the entire interval which dates from her mother-
hood to her death within sight of her native
shore, the greatness of her character cannot be
lost sight of or denied.

Three of Margaret Fuller's passionate loves
had been for children : the young Waldo Emerson, Pickie Greeley, and Hermann Clarke ; and
the depth of her feeling for her own child need
not be dwelt upon.   Yet she left him in what
she had every reason to fear were unsafe hands,
because she believed that the claim of a strug-
gling people was stronger than any other.   In
poverty, ill health, and desperate anxiety for the
little Angelo and her husband, she spent her
strength and affection in visiting hospitals, of
one of which she had charge, and in giving
cheer and encouragement to the allies of Young
Italy.   If her youthful aim had been mere self-

culture, the refining process of years had converted it into self-forgetfulness; if her early sphere of interests had been contracted, it had grown to embrace all human service. Strong, yet without health, her capacity for work was always astonishing; with an inborn love of ease and luxury, her acceptance of almost uninterrupted poverty was cheerful and sometimes grateful; and it is not easy to feel reconciled to the cutting-off of this renewed spirit from further participation in that human happiness for which she had always sighed, and which she had but just tasted.

Noyes, in his "History of American Socialisms," ascribes to Dr. Channing the inception of a plan out of which grew Brook Farm; and to W. H. Channing, his nephew, the fateful change from Associationism to Fourierism. There is some truth in both assertions, though of the most general character. Both the Channings had a courage and a loftiness of soul equal to the demands of any cause; but the lesser of the two had an overenthusiasm and lack of definiteness well calculated to wreck any project dependent on him alone to shape its course. He preached truths which, as Frothingham says, "were fundamental to him" though not to his hearers.

Born in 1810, he had, before he was twenty-five years of age, returned to Cambridge en-

William Henry Channing

riched by an experience of a few months'
preaching in the near West, but troubled with
his "disease of disproportionate speculation."
Shortly after this he sailed for Europe, and
there, as was the most natural thing in the
world for a troubled soul, felt the charm of
Romanism, which, had it "been as broad intellectually as it was grand sentimentally," would
have lulled his restlessness into acceptance.
During this trip his uncle wrote to ask him,
among other probing inquiries, if his new connection took him more from himself, or diminished his "selfish sensitiveness." After his
marriage in 1836, he undertook brief ministries
in New York and elsewhere, and then went to
Cincinnati. While still preaching there he
heard the clamor in Massachusetts over the
disintegration of the older Unitarianism. Persuaded that "Jesus Christ did not understand
his own religion"—another way of saying that
Christianity was not the religion of its founder
—he resigned a successful pastorate. "I walk
in a consciousness of unemployed force," he
wrote in 1840. Later came a series of meetings
in Brooklyn for a few months, and then a return
to New York. Some time in 1845 he left his
work in New York; and at about this period
arose a plan to take the place left vacant by
Parker, who had been invited to Boston, and who
was installed there on January 4, 1846. Chan-

ning had some reason to suppose that he would
succeed Parker, and doubtless was disappointed
in the failure of his hopes.   His nearness to
Brook Farm made it easy for him to harbor
there, and this he did during the summer of
1846.   He had left New York not only for the
sake of a settlement in West Roxbury, but also
to devote himself in part to the enterprise at
Brook Farm, and especially to serve the interests of the *Harbinger*, to which, however, the
total number of his contributions, to 1847, is
less than forty.   There is a general indefinite-
ness in regard to Channing's position at Brook
Farm; it is not sure when or how long he was
there; even his habitation is not clearly known.
His own purpose was to join the Association
actively with his family, but the wishes of his
wife, who shared happily the life of her husband
without accepting all his fervidness, stood out
against this plan, and Channing was therefore
an inspiration and an occasional presence, not a
constant factor.   The mention of his name is
frequent, though generally on some special occasion; he did not enter largely into the intimate
daily life, and was not in truth one of the sturdy
comrades of the barnyard and hayfield.   It is
evident from detached memoranda that Channing came to Brook Farm with no cool and logical convictions; he had not even a programme,
then as indispensable to a Reformer as his cloth-

ing. There was, however, no lack of an overflowing ardor which displayed itself even when an occasion might be lacking in inspiration. For the simple ritual of joining hands in dedication to the Universal Unity, Channing had a genuine relish, since he used it after Brook Farm had ceased to be; but it is impossible to infer how others were affected by a ceremonial which makes no solemn impression at a later day. Portentous phrases which once have thrilled earnest seekers sound hollow to an unappreciative generation. Such influence as Channing at this time was exerting is indeterminable, though he frankly espoused Brisbane's doctrines. Probably the momentary exaltation over his fine presence and his effective voice was great; then only did he assume prominence. Of his personality at this time Judge Mellen Chamberlain lately wrote: "After forty years I still see the light in his eyes; his wonderful voice thrills me yet, and to this day I ponder his ethical utterances." Channing was at no odds with his associates, and never quarrelsome; but he evidently felt, as he afterward admitted, that there was at Brook Farm too little spiritual atmosphere. He was well fitted in some respects, and aside from a want of organizing force, to impose a measure of religious discipline, not severe but sufficiently binding to commit the Association to a formal assent to the essential doctrines of Christ, to which, in fact, a nominal adherence was never denied. There would have been, at worst, no violent dissent, but, at best, some little indifference. So far as there may have been the suggestion of a vital religious life at Brook Farm, it is safe to admit that Channing sounded the dominant note. Dr. Codman recalls one Sunday afternoon on which the Associates were asked to join with Channing in a simple service in the grove near by. He speaks with deep feeling of the unpretentious beauty of the scene, and of the earnest idealist appealing to the young and hopeful spirits gathered apart from the strenuousness and realities of life. "Memory is the only photograph of it, and be assured the picture is a beautiful one." At times Channing would preach in the long parlors of the Pilgrim House.

With the burning of the Phalanstery came the real *coup de grâce*. Three years later Channing revisited Brook Farm "to close the eyes of that old friend, and say dust to dust, ashes to ashes." The conversion of the estate into a site for an almshouse, he calls a contrast between the "highest ideal and the lowest actual." Extravagantly but sincerely he continues: "Never did I feel so calmly, humbly, devoutly thankful that it has been my privilege to fail in this grandest, sublimest, surest of all movements";

but in 1871 he confessed that the experiment was "quite too tragic a one to be repeated," though for him its fragrance had never died. "Organize your townships," he held should have been the cry; yet, in spite of the disaster, Brook Farm was to him a "grand success as a college of social students."

On January 3, 1847, there was formed in Boston, under the lead of Channing, the "Religious Union of Associationists." A statement was drawn up, and ratified by the joining of hands of the persons present, among whom were seven of the most conspicuous Brook Farmers. All records of this Union cease after December, 1850; but as early as June of that year Channing, whose intensity in the cause was pathetic, took leave of his associates, thus practically ending an attempt to perpetuate one of the issues of the original movement. He then spent some months with the North American Phalanx, and as late as 1854 accepted membership with the Raritan Bay Union, the prospectus of which had been issued in 1852. Up to this time, kindly or not as the impression may be, Channing's relation to the ministry of the gospel stands forth as an avocation, and not as the absorbing labor of his soul. In August, 1854, he left a pastorate in Rochester, and in the fall went to Liverpool; henceforth he was identified with English life and religious thought. He remained, however, an American in spirit, as he afterward showed during the Civil War. One conspicuous achievement in England was his address in 1861, at Liverpool, on "The Civil War in America," in answer to a leader in the *London Times* indicting the Northerners as "savages." It demanded courage to meet boldly the uninformed and hostile state of public opinion in England at this time; but the loyal American proved himself on this occasion more radical on the problem of slavery than any other of his old fellow Associationists. The address was not devoid of a certain adroitness in its appeal to the essential unity of Great Britain and the United States as evinced by the cordial reception of the young Prince of Wales in America the year previous.

Channing returned to America to offer such devoted service as it was in his power to render during the war, as chaplain of Congress, and as a friend to the wounded and to the helpless freedmen. He revisited England during the war, and at its close went back to ally himself again with English institutions, on the solid foundations of which his tread became firm and assured. Several visits to his own country maintained associations here which he loved and had no intention of forsaking in spirit. In December, 1884, gradually worn out by an in-

creasing feebleness, he died peacefully, parting
with none of the ideals which had sustained him
during a life dedicated to almost every cause but
personal success.

No one was less dismayed by the Brook Farm
fiasco; and this was because, as in the case of
his uncle, William Ellery Channing, socialistic
tendencies were fundamental, and met with
no frustration from a temporary defeat. It
was this basic radicalism which led Channing
to walk off proudly, even defiantly, arm in arm
with a negro who was about to be restrained
by the officers of law in Washington just on
the eve of the Proclamation of Emancipation.
He was not dramatic in the doing of such
acts, but would always saunter into trouble
with a grace peculiar to nervous courage.
Underestimation of the importance of facts led
him to rush forward into easy traps. He was,
for instance, too readily betrayed into anti-
vivisection sympathies; he went dangerously
close to an espousal of the most vulgar of all
modern credulities, spiritualism, though it should
be said, somewhat in apology, that he possessed
to an unusual degree that force which is called
by the knowing "psychic." Frothingham says
that tables would run upstairs at Channing's
lightest touch; this phenomenon and others as
marvellous were later believed to be traceable
to unconscious muscular exertion. Channing

had shrunk from Garrison's uncompromising projects, but characteristically nourished an impractical hope that the conscience of both North and South could be uniformly roused to a pitch at which the whole nation, by some splendid abnegation, might snap the bonds of slavery. In all his errors, as in his successes, his courage and persistence were faultless. Emerson once inscribed an ode to him as:—

"The evil times' sole patriot."

Less approbative, but not a whit more unfriendly, was Theodore Parker's saying that "Channing hit the same nail every time; he hit it hard; but the head was downward; he never drove the iron in." What greater testimony to a stainless life could be paid, than was paid by Emerson when he allowed Channing to baptize his children, although he had previously refused to have the rite performed by any one because the children seemed to him purer than any minister whom he knew? Although Channing dealt in large themes, he wrote for the moment, and his writings have shared the fate of most inspirational work. At first he turned with some seriousness to the quiet courses of literature and philosophy. The preface to Jouffroy's "Introduction to Ethics," which he prepared for Ripley's "Specimens of

Q

Foreign Standard Literature," advocated the cause of French eclecticism, and encouraged the interdependence of psychology and the history of philosophy. He was favorably drawn to Cousin's method, and showed his appreciation of the ample use which Jouffroy made of Scotch and English thought. Pure philosophy was not long the business of so hurried a man, and Channing, once in the stream of life, was soon pulled away from these charms and floated easily into passing controversies. His enthusiasm for Christian Union was boundless. He formulated his principles on the question in 1843, and pleaded the "insufficiency of individual exertion"—naturally an unwelcome tenet to his friends the Transcendentalists. The matured plan was fairly tried in New York, but with small success. The people could not be brought to enjoy a Sunday service which was "wholly spontaneous," or a weekly meeting for the "frankest interchange of thought in conversation."

It is indeed strange how thoroughly Channing failed to lay hold on the organic sentiments of mankind. He was ill-adapted to conformity or to ritual, and was always peering out for further truth, as he had earlier shown that he would do in the last lines of "Ernest the Seeker," published anonymously in the first volume of the *Dial*. This religious novelette left the hero saying: "So, father, we must give up our free thought. You may be right. But I am not yet ready. I must examine fresh suggestions that come to my tent-door. They may be lepers to blast me with disease, but they may be also angels in disguise."

The month of April, 1844, which saw the last number of the *Dial*, saw also the close of the *Present*, which Channing began to edit in September, 1843. The reason assigned for the brief life of this magazine was that time and opportunity were needed for the preparation of the memoir of William Ellery Channing, his most signal contribution to American letters.

The *Harbinger* ceased in February, 1849, and in July of that year Channing began to issue the *Spirit of the Age*, which kept alive until April 27, 1850. With his irresistible openness the editor writes in the last number: "The paper is discontinued because, in brief, I am brain-sick — and it does not pay." It was fair to all manner of reforms, with none of which was Channing ever in complete accord. The title was a misnomer, else perhaps the paper might have lived. In taking farewell he admits that his burden "has been, is, and will be: to discharge, as best I can, the ungracious and ungratifying, the slightly appreciated, and rarely successful duties of a Reconciler."

His faith in a unity of religions **was** fast

when he delivered, in 1869, after intervening years of practical life following his fruitless editorships, a course of Lowell lectures on the "Progress of Civilization," in which he pressed the teleological argument to the full. These lectures he afterward used as material in discussions before the Summer School of Philosophy at Concord — that strange, flickering revival of the dialectic method on a Yankee soil. His astounding optimism never forsook him, and he never renounced hope in some form of socialism, though he came to distrust nationalism as the particular direction which reform might wisely take. He held, in earlier days, that socialism was realizable by virtue of the unitary tendencies of the race, and that the steps to attainment were Coöperation, Reconciliation, Equitable Distribution, Universal Culture, Association, and Harmony — large, bland words, powerless now to inspire, but once of a tranquillizing and assuring strength, when uttered by the musical voice of Channing, the hopefulest, but in memory the most shadowy, personality among the sanguine Brook Farmers.

The mental portrait is so interesting that over against it may properly be set Dr. Codman's description, and in his own words, of the outward Channing: "His figure was tall and stately, though rather slender. He carried himself finely, and walked with head erect.

His features were sharp cut, clean, and regular. His hair was dark and curling, and worn a trifle long for these days. His forehead was high and slightly retreating. His eyes were sharp and piercing, deeply set, with delicate dark eyebrows. His complexion was warm and brilliant, his beard closely shaven. He had a pleasant smile which, when it deepened, showed a fine set of white teeth. All of these physical signs were in his favor, but there was about his face, so handsome at times, an earnestness that seemed almost painful, when, devoted to the cause, he spoke with the burning, eloquent words he so often uttered."

It is arbitrary, no doubt, to consider with some fulness Margaret Fuller's relations to Brook Farm, and to pass Emerson briefly by. But Emerson always belonged to Concord; his identification with the place is so complete that the attempt would be forced to place him or his activities far outside the limits of that gracious town. From Concord he radiated his influences, and even when lecturing in the West he almost seems to have taken his peaceful surroundings with him; its calmness and virtue were reflected in his own attributes. Emerson went to Brook Farm, but seemingly in no other mood than when he went elsewhere. In return for this unbiased frame of mind, it is clear that the Associates heard

Ralph Waldo Emerson

him gladly, but met him only as he came,— the welcome guest or lecturer, as the case might be. There was no sitting at his feet; at a time when the little place overflowed with high spirits, and W. H. Channing held the emotions of all rapt as in a dream of heaven suddenly come to earth, Emerson's cool disrelish for discipleship was respected.

There was, indeed, some reason to think, before the experiment was begun, from his direct utterances, that Emerson might see it to be his duty and desire to join with Ripley; but his letter, probably written in the fall of 1840, firmly declined to take the step. Ripley's tone in his letter of invitation was so hopeful that it is hard not to suppose that Emerson had previously held forth some encouragement. After his answer there could no longer be any doubt, however, concerning his attitude. It is not discoverable if this declination was made public to the other members by Ripley; but, even had it been, their own decisions would hardly have been altered. Emerson was held by them, as by all intelligent men and women then and since, in due respect. His genius was recognized. By some, especially by the avowed Transcendentalists, he was regarded with veneration; but he was not really of them, as they hoed the field, washed the dishes, taught the children, and discoursed hopefully of the fast-coming regeneration of man. His was the sweet influence of the Pleiades which they would not attempt to bind; and he came and went, assenting to but never lauding their purposes, and caring little for their methods. Any spot less roomy than the universe or more contracted than Concord, could hardly have pleased him. Emerson's decision was partly based on the opinion asked of and given by Mr. Edmund Hosmer of Concord, an open-minded, wholesome character, answerable, one might fancy, to that description given of the "Farmer" by Emerson in his review of a Report of the Agricultural Survey of Massachusetts, and printed in the *Dial* for July, 1842. Hosmer distrusted on principle the "gentleman farmer," not because he was a gentleman, but because he was not a farmer; and he saw no practical results in a scheme which theoretically could not benefit the individual toiler.

It was consonant with Emerson's dignity to speak or write pleasantly or even gleefully of whatever was fairly open to tempered mirth. Ridicule or abuse was not in his nature. Some of the phases of Brook Farm life quietly amused him, and he did not hesitate to communicate his feeling to others. Just as he said of a certain meeting of the Transcendental Club that it was like "going to Heaven in a swing," so he playfully compared Brook Farm to a

"French Revolution in small." People would in turn enjoy themselves at his expense, but not in a loud-mouthed way. Ripley alone, of all men and women of that day, seems wholly to have escaped mild ribaldry. It was with Emerson a fair give and take. Once in a while he came in for abuse, as in the case of an unknown Mrs. Enge, of whom Mrs. Kirby speaks, who considered the philosopher a lunatic and in "a most deplorable state of mind and intellectual obliquity."

Anecdotes of his visits to the Farm are not numerous. Miss Russell, in one of her papers, recalls the pleasure which they always gave, and Mrs. Kirby, who says that he seemed "an integral part of the movement itself," tells of two women who had it in mind to walk to Concord on the chance of having a talk with him, arguing that "Emerson's impressions would be worth more to us than the clenched reasoning of others." A discerning woman is recorded as having said that it would not be difficult to confess to Mr. Emerson, "but he would be shocked at the proposition to take charge of even one soul." It was ever true of him that he felt the responsibility of his own selfhood too solemnly to be willing to intrude on another's personality. Having the extreme isolation of great courage, he disliked organization in itself. The impulse to arrange, classify, and coördinate has, in truth, more than a touch of the mediocre. The capacity to make things orderly is not the highest capacity because it is not creative but only adaptive. With the blithe hopefulness of Brook Farm for a new order which should subvert slow processes, a mind like Emerson's had little or nothing in common. He was as native as maize, and could not assimilate with much that was extravagant and foreign in the West Roxbury plan. Popular judgment, however, will hold him to have been a sort of godfather to the experiment, stooping now and then to smile benignly at the unsullied youth that dared what maturity and experience would have shunned. Into the fading memories of Brook Farm his name comes at times as a faint, pervasive aroma, outlasting any slight attachment which he may really have felt.

Alcott seems to have had a fostering care over these young people at Brook Farm, many of whom had heard, and possibly understood him. He, like Emerson, was approached with an invitation to be one of the pioneers, but no answer came from him so clear as that which reached Ripley from the honester and greater Emerson. In October, 1840, Alcott talked the project over at Emerson's house with Ripley and Margaret Fuller, and in his Diary spoke of "our community" without, however, assenting further to the scheme.

Amos Bronson
Alcott and
Charles Lane

In theory Alcott could certainly have made no such objections against Brook Farm as were offered by Emerson. Of reformers he announced in the " Orphic Sayings " that they " uproot institutions, erase traditions, revise usages, and renovate all things. They are the noblest of facts." He had not the genuine seer's distrust of compacted effort, else he would hardly have made the sorry venture at Fruitlands. As for the prime requisite of all accomplishment, did not this oracle proclaim that " labor is sweet . . . it exalts and humanizes the soul " ? Emerson, says Colonel Higginson, was " so far influenced by the prevailing tendency as to offer to share his house with Mr. Alcott and his family, while suggesting that other like-minded persons should settle near them." But this gregarious plan was to have been carried out at Concord, not at Brook Farm.

Alcott sincerely believed, no doubt, that Brook Farm, like Fruitlands, awaited "the sober culture of devout men." He sang the praises of toil; in dietetic reform he was the bravest of them all; and he would doubtless have welcomed the certainty of a home. Why, then, did he not go with Ripley? There is no sure answer, but we may, in fairness, suppose that he would have stayed long away from a project which involved three hundred days' labor in each year, with an average of fifty-four working hours to each week of six days. This philosopher would gladly have conversed under a noonday sun until the sweat poured down his face, but for physical toil he had no affinity. The nebular state of most projects was definite enough for Mr. Alcott.

He visited Brook Farm occasionally and held one or another of his talks. His gentle bearing and serenity may have quelled for the while the general effervescence; it was impossible not to love and even to respect him, so great seemed to be the distance between the vanities of actual life and the peculiar rehabilitation in his character of a calm belonging to centuries long past. One conversation at the Farm on "Insight" was thought, according to Mrs. Kirby, to have been "a trifle vague," though it persuaded young Newcomb that the sage was "steeped in Brahminism to the lips," as doubtless he was. Some of the hearers were so powerfully stirred by this address as to make the experiment of a vegetable diet.

A consideration of Mr. Alcott's merits and demerits is not here called for. By his own choice he did not belong to Brook Farm, but he was incidental to it. He contributed little to its existence, though a few such as he might have materially hastened its downfall. It is so easy a thing to gird at this man; so difficult in these days is it to see clearly his shadowy excel-

lences. Some of his earliest friends viewed him
with misgivings, and he was even called by
one of them "Plato Skimpole." To the day
of his death he encountered ridicule by reason
of what seemed his laziness, inefficacy, and
nebulosity. Almost all the anecdotes concerning him tend to derogation. The only way
in which to be just to him is deliberately to
search for what was admirable in the man
and hold fast to that. His school in Boston
was a good one, and well sustained while it
lasted. It was a concrete and applied Transcendentalism. Charles Lane had given him high
tribute in the third volume of the *Dial*, and before the melancholy fiasco at Fruitlands there
would have been little but respect, tempered by
smiles, to pay the well-disciplined and nobly
conceived Temple School, and the honorable
record which Alcott made in his visit to England. After he had dragged poor Lane down,
however, in their sorrowful little tragedy, Alcott
lost something which he never wholly regained.
Even at Concord distrust was felt, and Edmund
Hosmer alone, for a time, took him to his bosom.
Alcott went on bravely for many years, a sort of
living tradition; but there was no real advance,
and he was saying the same oracular things in
his simple manner, hopefully open to all truth
as he thought he saw it, until he came to sit, in
his advanced and easily flattered age, on the

platform where thundered, a score of years ago, that Malleus Hereticorum of New England orthodoxy, the Rev. Joseph Cook.

Alcott was in reality an innocent and harmless man; pure in heart, of an excellent humor, a learning wide but unprofound, and yet an absurdity to many, to some even an object of contempt. It is a difficult matter to keep one's hands wholly off Alcott's foibles. Had he lived in another township from Emerson, one might not have felt so keenly that he was always, and in quite a neighborly way too, tapping the spring of his friend's genius. The late Judge Hoar spoke perhaps for inarticulate Concord, when, meeting an acquaintance one day, he shot forth this savage conundrum and answer in the same breath: "What is the difference between Emerson and Alcott? One is a seer, the other a seer-sucker!" There is said to be but one step between the sublime and the ridiculous, and sometimes Alcott seems to have been that step.

Closely associated with Alcott for a time, and once, at least, but possibly oftener, making a visit with him to Brook Farm, was Charles Lane, an eccentric Englishman of ability and no small literary force. He had been manager of the *London Mercantile Price Current* and associated as editor of the *Healthian*, with Mr. Henry G. Wright, teacher of the Ham Com-

mon School, better known as the Alcott House
School, to which Mr. Alcott paid a famous visit
in 1842. Lane was of that extraordinary group
of English reformers so admirably described in
the *Dial* for October, 1842, consisting of John
A. Heraud, J. Westland Marston, Francis Barham, editor of the *Alist*, a monthly magazine
of "Divinity and Universal Literature," Hugh
Doherty, the ablest English representative of
Fourierism and editor of the *London Phalanx*,
and Goodwyn Barmby, editor of a penny
monthly, the *Promethean, or Communitarian
Apostle*, with "little fear of grammar and rhetoric before his eyes." Most famous of this
coterie was James Pierrepont Greaves, who had
died in March, 1842, after an abstention for
thirty-six years from fermented drinks and animal food, living mostly on "biscuit and water,"
and who was in England "a great apostle of the
Newness to many." Greaves's prime dogma
was the "superiority of Being to all knowing
and doing" — a dogma with which Alcott
would have been the last to quarrel; in fact,
they both were endued, as was said of Greaves,
with a "copious peacefulness." Among his
varied writings and activities, as a devout Pes-
talozzian, he composed "Three Hundred Max-
ims for the Consideration of Parents." Lane
was his literary executor.

Fresh from "Umbrageous Ham," which was

the first place to do Alcott substantial honor, and from these Syncretic Associationists, and all kinds of Notionists, Charles Lane came to this country as a sort of foreign importer of reforms, taking the place of Mr. Greaves, who before his death had seriously proposed a voyage to Boston. Lane himself was an original of the first water, and he naturally allied himself to whatever might be running counter to the world's practices. He wrote several articles for the *Dial*, — among them, and of particular interest here, a careful though brief study of Brook Farm, which was critical but not unsympathetic, and indicative of the interest which the writer had for the West Roxbury experiment. It is tempting to say more of the similarity, real though slight, between the movement in England, as chiefly represented by Greaves, and that on this side of the water, especially since little or no attention has ever been paid to this relation. But it must suffice to speak of Lane as introducing the knowledge of one movement to the other by means of his own strong personality.

Lane's economic ethics lay mainly in prescribing to himself what not to do — and this system of negation proved to be complicated and perplexing. He would have well-nigh solved the problem of earthly existence, had he possessed no outer skin to clothe, and no stomach to feed.

Avoidance consumed the larger part of each
day, and various encumbrances to a perfect life
gave him a great deal of trouble, because almost
every staple of commerce, such as wool, rice,
cotton, sugar, meat, both white and red, was an
offence to him. He would not use a horse, but
felt no scruple at riding his hobbies to the death.

Prosaic, sincere, and courageous in living up
to the articles of his faith, Lane was ready to
be victimized by any project which promised to
realize his dream of a "True Harmonic Association." An opportunity for complete disaster
soon came and was embraced. Fruitlands, a
farm of about one hundred acres in Harvard,
Massachusetts, and near the Shaker Community
so pleasantly described in the *Dial*, was bought
by Lane, who enlisted in this enterprise under
the flimsy banner of his friend Alcott. Ten
was the number of the Consociate Family, five
of whom were children. "Ordinary secular
farming" was not in the programme, which
planned to supersede the "labor of the plough
and cattle by the spade and the pruning knife."
Reliance was placed in the "succors of an ever
bounteous Providence," and in "uncorrupted
fields and unworldly persons." A "life of
gain" was to be scrupulously avoided. Father
Hecker's experience at Fruitlands is elsewhere
told, but the melancholy end must not be omitted
here. All of Lane's money was absorbed, and

in November, 1843, he wrote to Hecker thanking him for a barrel of wheat meal and submitting to him "a peck of troubles." He told how a large portion of the money which he invested went to pay old debts, and sought employment further south where he might support himself and his young son. His little all was "buried in the same grave of flowery rhetoric in which so many other notions have been deposited." This unhappy experience gives force to the severe definition of the Transcendentalists once put forth by the brilliant daughter of Father Taylor, that they "dove into the infinite, soared into the illimitable, and never paid cash!" W. H. Channing, in the *Present*, happily calls Alcott and Lane "the Essenes of New England," and compares them to "the more cheerful class of Therapeuts."

A few personalities, whose relations to Brook Farm were only tangential, imparted and gained some lustre by reason of this slight contact. Among those who added something to their own reputation from a supposed affinity for the Association was Brownson, but the only definite faith which he ever reposed in the place was shown when he put his son in the school; he was also instrumental in directing Hecker's steps toward West Roxbury in a wise and kindly fashion. He did Brook Farm a good turn, however, when he wrote in Novem-

Orestes
Augustus
Brownson

R

ber, 1842, an article for the *Democratic Review*,
in which he defended the simplicity of the
scheme as against Fourierism. His own visits
were not frequent, and it is hard to believe that
he was an especially welcome, though he was a
respected, guest. The little group which was
undergoing a process of Catholization was doubtless his main objective point; for the general
buoyancy and air of innocent joyance grated,
in all likelihood, on his rugged, honest seriousness.

Though early taught to walk in the usual
paths of New England Protestantism, at times
he "seemed to hold a spiritual intercourse with
the Blessed Mary and holy Angel Gabriel,"
showing the mystical temperament like his
friend Hecker, albeit heredity in both called for
no such manifestations. He strenuously labored
in many ways for the earthly well-being and happiness of mankind from 1828 until 1842, when
the trend toward Romanism definitely set in.
At first a Presbyterian, he soon veered to Uni-
versalism, and at the age of twenty-two became
a preacher of that sect. Then a great fervor
for social reform of many kinds came on him,
and lasted for some years. He felt directly the
powerful influence of Robert Owen, and indirectly that of William Godwin, of whose "Political Justice" Brownson says: "It has had
more influence on my mind than any other

book, except the Scriptures, I have ever read;" but Brownson-wise, after such an admission, he throws this barb: "there is scarcely a modern error that it does not contain." Erelong he found himself in coöperation with Frances Wright, Benthamite, emancipationist, and cultivated and effective orator, who, after her unhappy marriage with Darusmont, her factor, died in loneliness and poverty. "Poor Fanny" is Brownson's preface to a statement that she did "great harm, and the morals of the American people feel even to-day the injury she did them." It is hard not to see in the character of Priscilla in Brownson's "Spirit Rapper" — a dull, philosophic novel, written after he had made sure harbor — an embodiment of "Poor Fanny" Wright.

Brownson's next dissatisfaction was an alliance with the Workingmen's Party. Though retaining all his life an unaffected sympathy with "the more numerous classes," he soon gaged the futility of politics as a lever to proletarianism. Thereupon, as he says: "I resumed my old profession of preacher, though of what particular gospel it would be difficult to say." Unitarianism next attracted this restless being, and he became the friend of Channing, whom he evidently loved, but who was not "the great man many supposed him to be." In 1836, when actively began the ferment of which the

Brook Farm movement was one result, Brownson organized " The Society for Christian Union and Progress." Protestantism was already so distasteful to him as to give rise to a hope that he might reconstruct Catholicism, without regard, however, to the historic church. About this time Brownson published his " New Views of Christianity, Society, and the Church," of which he naïvely says : "it is the last word of the non-Catholic world." In 1838 followed his *Quarterly Review*, of which for five years he was almost as much author as editor. "Charles Elwood" (1840) is, as Ripley wrote in the *Dial*, "a slender thread of narrative made to sustain the most weighty arguments on the philosophy of religion." Such interest as this book may have to-day lies in the fact that it elaborates the theories of Cousin, then much engaging Brownson's attention. As he followed other illusions, so for a time he pursued St. Simonism from start to finish of its violent career. Brownson asserted, with his usual bluntness, that the " Mère Suprême " was too extreme a dogma to suit his "masculine dignity."

In 1840 Brownson awoke and found himself conspicuous if not famous. Allied for several reasons with the Democratic Party, he wrote in that year an essay on the laboring classes, in which he suggested the impairment, by political methods, of corporations and of the credit system. The Whigs, displaying an unexpected energy, printed his paper as a campaign document. The publication of this essay may have acted as a boomerang on his party, but it did Orestes Brownson a deal of good. It refreshed him as the deliverance from the Everlasting Nay refreshed Teufelsdröckh, and marked, as he says, "the crisis in my mental disease."

Out of his spiritual turmoil he gradually evolved, not without patience and a remarkable skill, a doctrine of Life: "that of the real infusion of a Divine element into human life," by which that life should be "supernaturally elevated and rendered progressive," — not so wide a digression, after all, from the upward path of his friends the Transcendentalists. Armed and comforted with this discovery, which he seems to have owed in part to Leroux, he sought at last the refuge toward which he had long been tending. Brownson, with all his audacity, hesitated at first in taking this step; but he went forward with good grace only to find that his vicissitudes of belief had made no favorable impression on a church which had become for him a crying necessity. In May, 1844, he sought the advice of Bishop Fenwick, and in October of the same year received the baptism and the sacraments of the Roman communion. He tells, not without dignity, in his apologia, "The Convert," of the relinquishment of his cherished

discovery, and of his entrance into the haven of
his salvation through a channel indicated by a
kindly but dogmatic pilot. There never can be
the least doubt as to the abiding satisfaction felt
by Brownson himself in his latest, and, as it
proved, his final decision. He trumpeted his
joy on the housetops, and from that time forward proclaimed the defects of Protestantism to
his heart's content. He despised the right of
private judgment — how freely he had used it!
he saw in the dialectic method, that powerful
adjunct of non-Catholic thought, not a philosophical method but a personal foe.

It is pathetic to have to recognize that Brownson is a really forgotten man, for at one time he
stood between contending forces a seemingly
powerful figure. But against the subtle individualism of the Protestant mind he contended with singularly little result. So doughty
a champion probably inspired his new friends
with a measure of dismay, while it may fairly
be doubted if he ever succeeded in winning a
notable convert to his own new way of thinking.
In this respect the contrast between him and
Father Hecker is striking. The unsympathetic
mind commonly regards him as a sort of ecclesiastical recidivist, who, having tried one form
of spiritual error, soon abandoned it, only to
seek another which in turn he would presently
repudiate. His conceit, of which he always

made frank acknowledgment, led him firmly to maintain that all this was consistent progress. The finest sentence he ever wrote, according to his acquaintance, Joseph Henry Allen, was one in which he upholds "that glorious inconsistency which does honor to human nature, and makes men so much better than their creeds." Just before the eventful change he had discontinued, in 1843, his *Quarterly*, and had immediately started another, which was continued until 1875 under the name of *Brownson's Quarterly Review*. He died in 1876.

Many considerations drove Brownson to his great affirmation, but one of them, considering the natural audacity of the man, deserves attention. It was nothing less than a strong desire for personal safety in eternity, or to use his own words: "because he would escape hell and gain heaven." He told Mr. Allen that on October 20, 1844, he "became a Christian." "But suppose," asked his questioner, with mild derision, "the process that made you a Catholic had stopped short at a certain point; suppose, for instance, that you had died on the nineteenth of October?" "I should have gone to hell," he replied, instantly and grimly. Like good Christian on his toilsome path to the City, though not afraid of an encounter, Brownson knew when it was time to use his legs.

It is unfortunate that so few traditions remain

of Brownson's contact with Brook Farm, for
he went there at the most critical moment of
his life, when, as a Brook Farmer once said,
"he walked backward into the Catholic church."
A few anecdotes indicate plainly that when
Brownson turned up the road leading to the
Hive he brought his disputatiousness with him,
and that he was apt to veer conversation around
to matters which interested him if nobody else.
Mrs. Kirby says, with her occasional tartness,
that he was "not the prince of gentlemen in
debate." "Do you approve of the priests of
the Inquisition roasting off the feet of children
under fourteen?" Cornelia asked. "Certainly,"
he replied, according to the same authority.
"It was better for them to have their feet
roasted off in this world than their souls to
be roasted forever in the next." No one can
doubt the sincerity of such a convert, but he
was just as sincere in his errors as in his assur-
ances, and this is a snare to the carnally minded.
Perhaps he himself has furnished an escape
from the dilemma when he says in the "Spirit
Rapper": "I never was so constituted as to
be able to strike a balance between truth and
falsehood, or to accept a principle and deny its
consequences."

Brownson certainly was not a "comfortable"
man; lack of breeding may cause a man to appear to be too honest. It would be interesting to

know what George Ripley thought of Brownson aside from the respect due his natural powers. Even in that gentle, strong heart must have been aroused the responsive opposition which the neglected pages of the great Catholic protagonist are still able to set going. One often-told anecdote must not be suffered to pass. At forty Brownson was obliged to study the classics the better to aid his ecclesiastical pursuits. He found much trouble with his Latin quantities. Ripley, so the story goes, dreamed that he went to confession, and that Brownson was the priest who should hear him. "Kneel, my son," said the priest, "and for penance repeat after me the fifty-eighth Psalm in the Vulgate." Ripley awoke, crying in his agony: "O Lord, my punishment is greater than I am able to bear." Another story evinces the feeble impression made by Brownson's vicissitudinary earnestness. A preacher once invited to the communion table the members of all Christian churches. Some one remarked that Brownson was the only person in the church who could "fill the bill."

Brownson was, in spite of his uneasiness, essentially conservative. "I had no natural relish for the Newness," he once said. How thoroughly he lacked a delicacy of touch is well seen in the chapter, "A Lesson in World Reform" in the "Spirit Rapper," where he crudely, and as he said, with "some degree of levity,"

serves up his old friends, the Transcendentalists, and other reformers, with a strong, coarse
relish. The noblest of them is plainly carica-
tured in Mr. Egerton, "a thin, spare man, with
a large nose, and a cast of Yankee shrewdness in
his not very handsome face." With his recession,
however, from early affiliations, died Brownson's
real potency, and certainly the picturesqueness
of his life. Powerful as he was in argument
and logical statement, he rested at last on a fal-
lacy. To one who once asked him how it was
that he felt so sure of his final decision, he replied: "When I was a Presbyterian, or a Universalist, or a Unitarian, or whatever I may
have been, I was sure each time that I was
right; but now I know that I *cannot* be wrong."

Brownson gives a portrait of himself in "The
Convert," which is probably as just as it would
be possible for one to give, in whom a desire of
self-exculpation was ever alive. It is worth quoting: "I am no saint, never was, and never shall
be a saint; but I always had, and I trust I always
shall have, the honor of being regarded by my
friends and associates as impolitic, as rash, im-
prudent, and impracticable. I was and am, in
my natural disposition, frank, truthful, straightforward, and earnest; and, therefore, have had,
and, I doubt not, shall carry to the grave with
me, the reputation of being reckless, ultra, a
well-meaning man, perhaps an able man, but so

fond of paradoxes and extremes, that he cannot be relied on, and is more likely to injure than serve the cause he espouses. So, wise and prudent men shake their heads when my name is mentioned, and disclaim all solidarity with me."

Theodore Parker's frequent visits to the Farm gave him a pleasant two-mile walk every few days across the fields from his house on Centre Street in West Roxbury, and furnished him at least wholesome exercise. Personal affection for George Ripley was the strongest element in his friendliness toward the institution, although his sense of humor was gratified by much that went on there, and perhaps his recognition of certain non-humorous aspects of the life may have been deeper than he cared to show. It was Parker's way to discover and laugh at the weakness of reforms to which he gave his support, and it is certain that he afforded some very practical assistance to Brook Farm.

The beginning of Parker's own perplexities was almost coetaneous with the establishment of Brook Farm, for his "Discourse of the Transient and Permanent in Religion," which was preached at the ordination of Mr. Shackford in South Boston, on May 19, 1841, occasioned the division of the religious community for and against him. Parker himself wrote of this discourse: "The sentiments in the South Bos-

Theodore Parker and Francis George Shaw

ton sermon had so long been familiar to me, I had preached them so often with no rebuke, that I was not aware of saying anything that was severe;" and at another time he affirmed, in regard to this same matter, that he had read it to a friend (presumably Ripley), who said it was the weakest thing Parker had written for a long while. As the defection of friends which ensued was a deeper grief to him because he was quite unprepared for it, so the stanch adherence of Ripley and a few others was a greater consolation. The obnoxious sermon was followed in the fall of 1841 by his lectures in the old Masonic Temple in Boston, "A Discourse of Matters pertaining to Religion," and the gulf was perceptibly widened by his utterances. The substance of these lectures, which were published in an enlarged form in the spring of 1842, was carefully talked over with Ripley, in whose literary and philosophical judgment he had the highest confidence. Parker's critical faculty was much less fine than that of Ripley, his scholarship was less accurate, and his intellectual temper less firm; but the two men were in close touch on most vital questions, widely as they differed in method, and were always mutually tolerant and sympathetic. That Parker had, at one time, some thought of Brook Farm as a temporary residence, he himself says in a letter to Dr. Francis, on June 24, 1842. Having spoken of the refusal of all but one or two of the Boston Association of Ministers to have any ministerial intercourse with him, and of the likelihood of his having to desert the pulpit, he writes: "I mean to live at Spring Street, perhaps with Ripley;" but the emergency passed, his parish sustained him, and for another year he worked hard in behalf of liberal Christianity. Signs of exhaustion began to develop in the summer of 1843, and in September, through the thoughtfulness of one of his friends, he went to Europe for a year. When he came back to the toil that he loved, the continuing trouble with his head, which debarred him from the arduous labor that he would have preferred, left him free to see much of his friend Ripley. This was the last winter in which they were to meet often and freely; for in December, 1845, Parker accepted a call issued by a new society which held services in the Melodeon — the 28th Congregational Society — and very soon after left West Roxbury for an absorbing, troubled, but valiant career. The attachment between the two men ended only with Parker's death in 1859. After Ripley went to New York they saw little of each other, but each followed the other's course with unabated interest. Parker wrote to Ripley in the early part of the last year of his life: "I count your friendship as one of the brightest spots in my life." It is quite possible that while they had strengthened and supported each other, Parker may have benefited more from the friendship. As men, they were equally honest; but Ripley could give and take a rebuke or a criticism more generously than Parker; he could see his antagonist's side of an argument more clearly than Parker; and his caution often placed a wholesome check on Parker's impetuosity.

Parker made merry over the dress of the community; his congregation, however, always numbered a fair percentage of Brook Farmers, who shared his religious sentiments, and felt the humanity beneath his blunt self-assertion. His library was freely opened to the youth of the neighborhood; but it is not known how freely this offer was accepted, for hardly a person remains there to-day who could have come under his influence at that time. The little church still stands, having been temporarily rescued from the destroying hand of improvement by the private means of one who will, it is hoped, preserve this humble monument to the memory of Theodore Parker's early struggles for religion as opposed to theology.

Had Emerson and Parker connected themselves with Brook Farm, the first bringing his genius, and the other his religious nature, they would have effectually added to the intellectual equipment, strong already in Ripley's philo-

sophical attainments, Dwight's earnestness for
music, and Mrs. Ripley's and Dana's devotion
to the school.   No ultimate results were changed
by their not joining these allied forces; yet had
they become Brook Farmers, the humanities
would have been handsomely represented in a
sort of Agrarian University.

There ran in Parker's veins the blood of a
hard-working, farming race, shrewd to discover
the impractical side of a character or an undertaking.   Parker may, through this inheritance,
have reflected the general opinion of the inconspicuous yeomen of West Roxbury, in his
standing off a little from his friends at the
Farm — not hostilely, but somewhat quizzically
and disdainfully, as a countryman might, who
knew himself to dig and delve on New England
soil.   Besides the honest folks who mainly composed the population of the town, there were
several families of refinement and great respectability who lived there, not exactly *en grand
seigneur*, but preserving the aloofness so characteristic of our incomprehensible democracy —
always with the people, never of them.   Among
these families were the Shaws, the Russells,
and a few others.   Mr. Francis George Shaw,
one of the most estimable of these local patri-
cians, early gave his hand to Brook Farm.
If, like Parker, he entertained his own reserved
opinion as to the venture, he went further

than Parker in extending sympathy. From gradually formed social intimacies grew deep and lasting friendships. Years later Curtis married Shaw's daughter, the sister of Robert Gould Shaw, West Roxbury's loved and honored hero. of the Civil War. Another daughter, Ellen, married General Francis Channing Barlow. Shaw is best remembered for excellent English renderings of several foreign works of note, especially of George Sand's "Consuelo," which first appeared in the *Harbinger*. Of him, shortly after his death, Curtis, with the usual serenity and delicacy of the Easy Chair, wrote: "He was allied by sympathy more than by much previous actual association with the founders of Brook Farm. But when they chose the site for their enterprise not far from his house, he was soon in the pleasantest relations with the leaders, for their spirit and purpose were in harmony with his own." He was as useful to George Ripley as to his nearer neighbor, Theodore Parker, and his friendliness to the Association was the more significant by reason of his social conservatism. Like a few other reserved men of his standing, he was a radical on the question of slavery, and was a friend to such leaders as Garrison, when this sort of allegiance cost something. He instinctively shunned extravagance of life, but his home always preserved its individuality. He had sympathy and heartiness, and an undying

"devotion to the well-being of other men."
"Kindly, but firmly, he protected his own seclusion, and he permitted no man, in Emerson's phrase, to devastate his day."

The appearance of Cranch at Brook Farm was always an event. This uncircumscribed genius, by his very presence, made everybody forget the dilapidated condition of the parlor furniture at the Hive; and by his singing, which he himself accompanied either with guitar or piano, he contrived to infuse an atmosphere of affluence into the place which lent grace and elegance to this little world. Curtis says that he became simultaneously acquainted with Cranch and Schubert; for Cranch had made a manuscript copy of the "Serenade," which he sang with such deep feeling as to move sensibly his audience; and when, on his first visit to the Farm, he sang the ballad "Here's a health to ane I lo'e dear," tears were the tribute from some who heard him. His powers of entertainment were almost unlimited: he had a good baritone voice; he played piano, guitar, flute, or violin as the occasion came; he read from his own poems or travesties; and his ventriloquism, which embraced all the sounds of nature and of mechanical devices, from the denizens of the barnyard to the shriek of the railway locomotive, held the younger members spellbound with amusement, or led to loud expressions of approval.

Christopher Pearse Cranch

s

In personal appearance he was of the picturesque type of beauty, with much dark curling
hair, a broad forehead, delicately cut features,
and great sensitiveness of expression.   Tall,
slight, and graceful, he was an alluring presence
at all times, and especially when, as at Brook
Farm, his imagination was kindled and his sympathies strongest.

Cranch had been graduated from Columbian
University in 1832, at the age of nineteen, and
had then gone to the Harvard Divinity School,
where he formed a friendship with Dwight, who
was in the class below him, Cranch's class being
that of 1835.   His ministry had been brief, for
he abandoned the pulpit in 1842 in order to
study art abroad.   To this profession he devoted
the remainder of his life, making his American
home in New York until some time before his
death, when he went to Cambridge, where he
died in 1892.   Much of his life had been spent
in Europe, largely in Rome and Paris, and his
painting was distinctly above the average.   His
poetical contributions to the *Harbinger* are graceful and give full evidence of his simplicity, his
love of beauty, and his buoyant hopefulness.
His sympathies were strongly with the Transcendental movement and with Brook Farm as
an outcome of that movement.   If, perhaps, it
was true of him that versatility was fatal to
achievement, it is also true, as Curtis wrote in

1892, that " he was of that choice band who are always true to the ideals of youth, and whose hearts are the citadels which conquering time assails in vain."

Few steps in the direction of social progress in Boston, between 1830 and 1890, were taken without obtaining the pronounced support of Elizabeth P. Peabody. She loved reforms, not indiscriminately, to be sure, but as the legitimate progeny, varying in worth, of a common sentiment. Every moral effort, to her mind, deserved encouragement, and throughout her long and honorable life we find her a stanch friend of the negro and the Indian, a student on subjects ranging from Spiritualism to the Kindergarten, a writer, and a publisher of books. Her rooms on West Street, where she had a circulating library, were the resort of the men and women who, though of the literary clan, longed for action; and the early Brook Farmers and their friends — Ripley, Parker, Dwight, Samuel Robbins, Brownson, and Burton — frequently met here. Margaret Fuller, whom Miss Peabody sincerely admired, held her Conversations in these rooms, in part of which Dr. Nathaniel Peabody, Elizabeth's father, kept a homœopathic drug-shop. Her passion for knowledge was strictly impersonal, for she was not a whit more zealous to obtain it for herself than to direct others to it. James Freeman

Elizabeth Palmer Peabody

Clarke has said that she "was always engaged
in supplying some want that had first to be created." The little shop on West Street was allo-
pathic indeed in the dispensing of cures for
social and moral ills.

At sixteen she began to teach, her first pupils
being her sisters Mary and Sophia, afterward
Mrs. Horace Mann and Mrs. Nathaniel Hawthorne. When she was eighteen she met Emerson and induced him to give her lessons in
Greek, for which the teacher later refused to be
paid because he thought he could teach her
nothing. Both these young creatures were shy,
Emerson being a year older than herself, and
not even a "chatting acquaintance" came from
their studies. She was Channing's literary assistant for a time, and in 1834 gave some instruction in Mr. Alcott's Temple School, besides
taking down his conversations and publishing
them afterward as the "Record of a School."

This intimate transcendentalist acquaintance,
joined with her delight in all spiritual agitations,
naturally enough awakened her interest in Brook
Farm; but she was too busy a woman to pay
frequent or long visits to the community; her
occasional coming, however, was counted as an
especial pleasure by her friends there. She
did not regard the Farm as a retreat in which to
forget the demands of the world upon her, as
Margaret Fuller frankly confessed to doing, but

as an opportunity for enlarging her moral and intellectual experience. Perhaps her best service to the Association was effected through some of her articles in the *Dial*, where, in 1842, appeared her "Glimpse of Christ's Idea of Society" and her "Plan of the West Roxbury Community," both written without a trace of the partisan spirit. When, in 1844, she came to write of Fourierism at Brook Farm, she preserved the same lofty and unprejudiced attitude, although there is little doubt that her feeling was against the change. One sentence of this article is, to be sure, a formidable challenge, but even in this the reader perceives the judicial above the personal tone: "The question is whether the Phalanx acknowledges its own limitations of nature in being an organization, or opens up any avenue into the source of life that shall keep it sweet, enabling it to assimilate to itself contrary elements and consume its own waste; so that, phœnix-like, it may renew itself forever in greater and finer forms."

Her intellectual vigor is all the more striking because she was naturally desultory and dreamy, and because her tendency to scatter her forces was strong. Fortunately the object of her late, and perhaps greatest interest, the Kindergarten, has achieved permanent and visible results. The Elizabeth Peabody House, on Chambers Street in Boston, reared by a body of teachers

in whom her enthusiasm had kindled a deep
response, is especially dedicated to the training
of the children of the poor by kindergarten
methods.

Miss Peabody was the original of Miss Birds-
eye in " The Bostonians " of Henry James — the
charming old lady who " would smile more if
she had time "; and she was in her later life
known among her friends as "the Grandmother
of Boston," because she once filled the character
in an exhibition of Mrs. Jarley's Waxworks.
For some years before her death she was totally
blind, but this affliction hampered her less than
would be supposed.   One incident of the ses-
sions at the Concord School of Philosophy shows
the respect in which she was universally held.
Two young reporters who were sent out to
write up the proceedings of one day were instructed to make all the fun they chose of anybody but Miss Peabody — a creditable restraint
in the annals of the daily press.   When she
died, on January 3, 1894, in her ninetieth year,
it was with her mental power almost undimin-
ished, and her childlike and effusive spirit un-
changed.

CHAPTER VI

THE CLOSING PERIOD

THE principal factors of the latter days The "Har-binger" were two. One was the introduction of a form of Fourierism, as modified by Mr. Albert Brisbane; the other was the *Harbinger*, which was not only the official organ of Fourierism in this country, but a literary feature in the annals of Brook Farm, so important as to deserve special attention, both on its own account and in connection with the *Dial*. The *Dial* and the *Harbinger* had few points of resemblance, but they belonged to the same intellectual family. Neither of them espoused directly the cause which it represented. The *Dial* was edited and conducted by the Transcendentalists of Boston and Concord, but it contained no direct advocacy of the cult. This proved a source of strength, and has made the *Dial* an integral fragment in the history of American letters. The *Harbinger* devoted itself to the cause of Association and Fourierism, neglecting almost wholly the immediate and urgent interests of Brook Farm. This policy, which was deliberate, turned out to be a mistake, for it would have been legitimate for an "organ," such as this paper unquestionably was, to inform its friends and the public generally regarding matters in which much interest, to say nothing of curiosity, was constantly manifested.

The affinity between the *Dial* and Brook Farm alone may here claim attention. When the *Harbinger* was born, the older magazine was already dead; but almost all who had written for the *Dial* wrote also for the new journal. Several of the contributors to the transcendental quarterly became active Brook Farmers. In volume two of the *Dial* appeared three papers: one, entitled "Prophecy, Transcendentalism, Progress"; the second, "A Glimpse of Christ's Idea of Society"; the third, "Plan of the West Roxbury Community"—the last two by Miss Peabody; in volume three, one paper entitled "Fourierism and Socialism," introducing another by Brisbane; and in volume four a paper on "Brook Farm" by Charles Lane, and one on "Fourierism" by Miss Peabody—all important contemporary matter bearing directly or indirectly on the history and the conditions of the Association, from a friendly but not always approbative source, and constituting the only powerful influence outside itself, except the *Tribune* in New York, which Brook Farm ever had.

The ceasing of the *Dial* and the *Present* left a clear field for the *Harbinger*. In a little less than fifteen months later, on June 14, 1845, appeared the first number. The new paper could not have been started during the life of either of these precursors, for the reason that there would have been no room for it; it could only have paralleled the philosophical and literary attempts of the one, and the reform spirit of the other. Ripley did, however, seize one advantage in making the *Harbinger* a recognized organ of a far larger purpose than the financial welfare of a single and local experiment. There was some reason to hope for a moderate success in advocating the cause of Association. The country at large was taking an uncommon interest in this, one of the absorbing questions of the time. If there were journals already devoted to social reform, no other had so wide a programme, so able a corps of writers, or so good a vantage point. The *Harbinger* was also to occupy the field left open by Brisbane's paper, the *Phalanx*, which ceased to appear in 1845.

With number one of the fifth volume, in June, 1847, the *Harbinger* was transferred to the American Union of Associationists, and continued to be published in New York until February, 1849, when it died. Its successor was Channing's *Spirit of the Age*, begun in July of that year and ended in April, 1850. The *Har-*

binger was a generous quarto, with three columns to a page, of no beauty of type or paper; it was less attractive than the *Dial*, although it was reputably and clearly printed. It appeared weekly, and its subscription price was two dollars a year in advance, and one dollar for six months. A single copy could be bought for six and a quarter cents. There were several agents at various times, particularly in New York, Boston, and Cincinnati. The advertisements were very few. Ripley's introductory notice in the first number was marked by great moderation, without a word relating directly to Brook Farm. The good of all mankind was the keynote: "our motto is the elevation of the whole human race, in mind, morals, and manners, and the means . . . orderly and progressive reform. . . . We shall suffer no attachment to literature, no taste for abstract discussion, no love of purely intellectual theories, to seduce us from our devotion to the cause of the oppressed, the down-trodden, the insulted and injured masses of our fellow men." In regard to the constituency Ripley closes: "We look for an audience among the refined and educated classes . . . but we shall also be read by the swart and sweaty artisan." The artisan and the cultured were ready to hand at Brook Farm, not so much to read as to make the *Harbinger*, which owes its existence to this combination. It was a necessity, in fact, that

some such project be undertaken to provide
work for the incoming members, skilled to what
they had already learned to do, and of little use
in the farm work. The Association could have
furnished intelligence, but the Phalanx alone
provided technical skill; and there was enough
literary capacity left over from the early Associates to furnish copy for the Printers' Group.
So far, then, it was not an unwise business
undertaking, but its results were more far-reach-
ing than was anticipated. It not only gave immediate work to compositors and pressmen, but
it brought forward in a definite way literary apti-
tudes which needed soil for a start, and which
grew sturdily after the paper had stopped.

It is not safe to say how many copies of the
Harbinger were disposed of. In number five
of volume one it is stated that a circulation of
one thousand had been reached, and that new
names were "coming in every day." There is
little probability that a distribution of two
thousand copies was ever attained. Ripley
was editor-in-chief, and even after the paper
was transferred to New York, he continued in
his position, at a salary of five dollars a week,
while Dwight and W. H. Channing were retained as Boston contributors. The list of
writers was strong: from New York were eight
men, — Brisbane, Channing, Cranch, Curtis,
Godwin, Greeley, and Osborne Macdaniel; from

Brook Farm, five, — Ripley, Dwight, Dana,
Orvis, Ryckman; from Boston, six, — Higgin-
son, Story, Otis Clapp, Dr. Walter Channing,
W. F. Channing, and James Freeman Clarke;
also Lowell from Cambridge, Shaw from
West Roxbury, Whittier from Amesbury, J. A.
Saxton from Deerfield, A. J. Duganne from
Philadelphia, and E. P. Grant from Ohio. There
were other contributors, among them Allen and
Pallisse of Brook Farm, W. E. Channing, the
poet, Hedge, Stephen Pearl Andrews, S. D.
Robbins, and a few more.

The heaviest articles and editorials came from
Ripley, Dana, and Brisbane; and now and then
Dwight would write something on Association
or an allied topic, which seemed a little more
luminous than the downrightness of Ripley, or
the fierce, polemic tone of Dana, who, besides
these serious efforts, did many book reviews,
spoken of elsewhere, and a number of poems
which had force and earnestness, though little
sweetness. Dwight naturally confined himself
mainly to musical criticism and the extolment
of the art which he loved so devotedly. Mr.
Cooke goes so far as to say that the *Harbinger*
"became one of the best musical journals the
country has ever possessed."

A valuable addition to the musical feature
was the correspondence of Curtis from New
York. The poetry was mainly furnished by

Cranch, Lowell, Story, Higginson, Duganne, Dana, and Dwight — the two latter also translating some poems from the German. Translations were an important feature. George Sand's "Consuelo" and her "Countess of Rudolstadt" were admirably put into English by neighbor Francis G. Shaw. To think of the *Harbinger* is to recall Shaw's translations. There were occasionally anecdotes of a humorous nature. It would even be profitable for one hunting for early specimens of American wit to run through the few volumes of the *Harbinger*. Boston and its vicinity was not then so radiant with jocularity and spontaneous joy that this feature of the *Harbinger* should be passed by. These amenities grew scarcer as the faces at Brook Farm grew longer, and the later pages are wholly given over to serious things.

Of the articles, Dwight wrote three hundred and twenty-four, Ripley three hundred and fifteen, Dana two hundred and forty-eight, and Channing thirty-nine. The printers of the *Harbinger* deserve a word. One was Butterfield, who married Rebecca Codman. He was a tall, handsome man, and was familiarly known as "Hero." The other was "Grandpa" Treadwell.

There are published to-day, where once the *Harbinger* had its home, three Lutheran church papers: one, fortnightly, in the Lettonian language, one in Esthonian, and one in German. Thus the literary traditions of Brook Farm are still locally maintained.

When Charles Fourier, the son of a French linen-draper, died in 1837, at the age of sixty-five, his theories were not well known in this country. In an article on Fourierism, which appeared in the *Dial* for April, 1844, Miss Peabody wrote that the "works of Fourier do not seem to have reached us," and that she had entertained "remembrances of vague horror" connected with his name. To criticise or to elucidate Fourierism now is unnecessary. Admirably did Emerson penetrate the mesh when he said that Fourier "had skipped no fact but one, namely, Life," and that he "carried a whole French revolution in his head, and much more." The single point of interest is to understand how such a theory could have found even partial acceptance with Horace Greeley, Parke Godwin, Margaret Fuller, George Ripley—all possessed of sound mind and disposition—to say nothing of the lesser known Fourierists, like Byllesby, Skidmore, and others. Even in London, where men are hard-headed, the *Phalanx*, under the editorship of Hugh Doherty, was making good headway, first as a weekly, then as a monthly journal. To Albert Brisbane belongs the responsibility of importing the Frenchman's doc-

Albert Brisbane and Fourierism

trine to this country, and of infecting the shrewd Yankee intelligence with its allurements. Horace Greeley was the ablest and easiest victim; but it was not long before the staff of the *Tribune*, which first appeared in April, 1841, was well infused with Fourierism.

Brisbane was born in 1809, at Batavia, N. Y., and spent his early manhood in study in various parts of Europe, and in travelling extensively there, as well as in Turkey and Asia Minor. Of sound education and good intellectual training, he was also of an honest, kindly, and rather innocent character. Sympathetic by nature, he was impressed by what he believed to be the unnecessary sufferings of humanity, and was deeply stirred by the injustice of the social system. In this mood it was easy for him to become profoundly attracted by Fourier's Association and Attractive Industry, which promised all that the fondest dreamer for better days could hope. His interest expressed itself through his "Social Destiny of Man, or Association and Reorganization of Industry," published at Philadelphia in 1840, when he was about thirty years of age. This was followed by "A Concise Exposition of the Doctrine of Association," which, it may be supposed, had the most immediate effect on the members at Brook Farm. He was in moderate but not dependent circumstances, and would prosecute no business for merely personal gain. Though scornful of trivial discussions, he was devoid of fanaticism and intolerance. It was his opinion that America, not France, was the true field for this gospel; though an American, he lacked the national quality of humor, the possession of which would have saved him some Gallic extravagances. Emerson was amused to see that Brisbane in his earnestness made everything reducible to order, — even "the hyæna, the jackal, the gnat, the bug, the flea, were all beneficial parts of the system"; but it took "1680 men to make one Man." Respecting Brisbane's seriousness, Arthur Sumner tells of a group of Brook Farmers lying out in the moonlight. "What a heavenly moon!" said one. "Miserable world! Damned bad moon!" was poor Brisbane's reply. The "Ay, it's a sad sicht," of the dyspeptic Carlyle as he looked with Leigh Hunt at the starry heavens hardly equals this cosmic despair.

Distrusting with Fourier all cant regarding the "progress of humanity," Brisbane fell back, like the Master, on the perfection of nature. He confined himself in his writings to the elucidation and modification of the social schemes of Fourier, leaving superterrestrial regions fairly well alone. "Philosopher Brisbane," as the *New York Herald* was pleased to call him, was sincere, but he had certain dangerous mental qualities. Miss Russell, who was never con-

verted, says that he had the power to answer
objections, but not to convince. He dealt in
futures, and could, by his eloquence and sense
of expansion, make listeners fancy that the
great reformation had already begun. That
he could have thus influenced unemotional
Ripley is strange indeed. One gets the impression that Brisbane was not an "interesting" personality, though he had an intellectual
face and forehead. He wore a closely trimmed
beard, and was of good height. His voice
was rapid and not soothing, though full of
earnestness. He died on May 1, 1890.

Brisbane's first important proselyte was the
radical editor of the *Tribune*. The outward
appearance of Horace Greeley was that of
some wondering Moses at the fair, ready to be
duped by any fakir; but he was in most concerns shrewd and cautious. Had there not
been within him a heart quick to respond to
suffering, perhaps he would not have embraced
the doctrines of Brisbane so readily. While
serving laboriously on one of the committees appointed in the city of New York to relieve the
hardships of the winter of 1838, he fell in with
much distress, for which he felt, like Brisbane,
that there must be an alleviation if not a
remedy. To bring this about he wrote some
articles for the *New-Yorker*, which attracted
the notice of Brisbane, who was then bringing

T

back with him from abroad a plan for the
rehabilitation of the universe, and who found
Greeley ready to listen even to news from the
moon.   By lectures and conversations Brisbane
began to make headway. Six months after
the *Tribune* appeared there was a formal notice
of one of Brisbane's lectures, followed a few
weeks later by warmer commendation.   Early
in the next year a column on the first page of
the *Tribune*, the daily and weekly circulation
of which then exceeded twenty thousand copies,
was purchased by a few votaries with the understanding that it was to be filled by the pro-
ductions of Brisbane's pen, pushed, as the *Dial*
says, "with all the force of memory, talent,
honest faith, and importunacy."   This column
was faithfully employed, though not always
daily, until the middle of 1844, when the writer
revisited Europe.   Like the rest of Brisbane's
writings, these contributions make hard reading
to-day ; they were doggedly sincere, never by
accident brilliant, and they finally did win attention.   Fourierism was at last in the air, and it
was known that Greeley was infected by it.
Not that he or his paper really indorsed Fourierism, but they encouraged it.   Greeley was
too radical to trust any scheme absolutely.   It
is corroborative of the progress which Fourierism was really making, particularly in the city
of New York, that the Society Library, a highly

conservative institution, should have opened its
rooms in 1844 to lectures by Godwin, Greeley,
and W. H. Channing.

There soon began attacks, personal and general, from certain papers, in particular from the
Rochester Evening Post, the *New York Express*,
and from the *Courier and Enquirer*, the most
powerful of all antagonists. In the fall of 1846,
when about two hundred thousand Americans
are said to have acknowledged the name of
Fourierists, there was opened a battle royal
between the quills of Horace Greeley and Henry
J. Raymond, formerly on Greeley's staff, and
then writing for Colonel James Watson Webb's
Courier and Enquirer. It was occasioned by
a letter written by Brisbane on his return from
Europe in 1846, to the *Courier and Enquirer*, but
printed in the *Tribune*. For six months and
in twenty-four articles, afterward gathered into
book form, raged this spirited and able controversy. Parton, who never wrote a dull line, has,
with all his best vivacity, condensed the debate
into a few pages of his campaign life of Greeley.
The contest ended with a generally admitted
triumph of skill on the part of Raymond over
Greeley's earnestness. The *Tribune* acknowledged no defeat, except by a sudden silence after
the last argument by Raymond on May 20, 1847.
There were occasional, and not unfriendly, allu-
sions to Fourierism, but the *Tribune*, as an

active journal, withdrew its approval. If, however, Greeley no longer waved the banner of
Fourierism, he did not relinquish his efforts for
social amelioration. As late as 1868 he reaf-
firmed a faith in Association and rejected Communism as at war with one of the strongest
and most universal instincts.

Greeley took a deep and practical interest in
Brook Farm; several of his intimate and trusted
friends were there, and he was glad to sustain
them by kindly encouragement in the *Tribune*,
and by an occasional visit. Miss Russell relates
amusingly the coming of an apparition which
proved to be Greeley, not in disguise, but
simply his astonishing self. "His hair was
so light that it was almost white; he wore a
white hat; his face was entirely colorless, even
the eyes not adding much to save it from its
ghostly hue. His coat was a very light drab,
almost white, and his nether garments the
same." This Apostle of Light, however odd
his personality, was welcome to the community to which he was never disloyal, though his
heart was more with the North American
Phalanx, a visit to which was easier for so
busy a man. Little as they saw of him,
Greeley's good will was valued by the Brook
Farmers, none of whom is known to have held
Emerson's opinion that he was both coarse and
cunning. Through no fault of his own, Greeley

was probably an injury to the West Roxbury
community. It was his misfortune — a misfortune which followed him to his tragic end — to
excite marked political antagonisms, and it was
natural that such interests as he espoused should
come also under the ban.

How happened it that Brook Farm, after two
years of institutional life, which gave no distinct
outward evidence of failure, came to change
from an Association of individuals into a
Phalanx modelled in part after the plan of
Fourier? The various recollections say only
in a dim way that at about this time there
was much talk of a change, and that finally it
was effected, principally through the influence
of Brisbane. Brisbane was welcomed with the
heartiness so generally shown at that time by
each phase of reform to every other. Even
the *Dial* for July, 1842, opened its columns to
Brisbane, whom it greeted as an honest man
in "a day of small, sour, and fierce schemes."
In the *Present* for October, 1843, Channing
held out a generous hand to him, though saying with his wonted frankness that Fourier
must be held fallible in many things, and that
a "science of Universal Unity is not for this
generation." This is curious when we consider how often the phrase was subsequently
on Channing's own lips. In the same number
of the *Present* there is announced a call,

signed by J. A. Collins, N. H. Whiting, John
Orvis, and J. O. Wattles, for a meeting at the
Community in Skaneateles, New York, on
October 14 and 15, 1843, in the interest of a
reorganization of the social system by a community of property and interest throughout
the country. This was hardly more than a
straw; but in the December number of Channing's journal there was a call for a convention of the friends of Social Reform in New
England and elsewhere, to be holden in Boston,
on December 26 and 27, 1843. Among the
signers of this call were three members of the
Northampton Association; five persons from
Lynn, Massachusetts; seven from Boston;
one from Lowell; F. S. Cabot, John Allen,
George C. Leach from Roxbury, Massachusetts
(all Brook Farmers), and L. W. Ryckman, Brook
Farm. It was felt that the time was ripe for
testing Fourier's theory of Attractive Industry
and of Passional Harmonies. Channing warmly
commended this call; while admiring Fourier's
accuracy, "gorgeous and stupendous imagination," conscientiousness, and other brave virtues,
he sent out a word of warning against his sweep-
ing censure of society, his arrogance toward
criticism, and his "morbid impatience with what
he thought error, hypocrisy, or pretension."
Evidently on December 15, 1843, neither Channing nor the more prominent members of Brook

Farm were committed on paper to Brisbane and Americanized Fourierism. In the next number of the *Present* (January, 1844) is a full story of the convention, which lasted over from the last week of December into the first week of January, and marked, in Channing's words, "an era in the history of New England." It proved to be a veritable love-feast of the associations at Northampton, Hopedale, and Brook Farm ; it was plain that the drift of the convention as a whole was Fourierward. Not forgetting his former strictures, Channing said that it at last seemed to him that Fourier had "given us the clew out of our scientific labyrinth and revealed the means of living the law of love." Association was upheld, but there was some passing friction between the communal and associative ideals. The resolutions indorsed Fourier and hoped to see a "test of the actual working of his principles."

On January 18, 1844, appeared a second edition of the constitution of the Brook Farm Association, printed in the March issue of the *Present*, and prefaced by an important statement signed by Ripley, Pratt, and Dana. After summarizing the existing conditions and advantages of the Farm, they continued as follows : " With a view to the ultimate expansion into a perfect Phalanx, we desire without any delay to organize the three primary departments of labor, namely, Agriculture, Domestic Industry, and the Mechanic Arts." This change, so radical and so fateful, was thus definitely announced. A decision was certainly reached with remarkable promptness after the December convention, but there is reason to suppose that it had been for some time slowly forming in the minds of the real leaders.

Brisbane was deeply interested in this change, which his influence, no one knows how directly, did so much to effect. He lectured and visited at Brook Farm, and at one time remained there for several months. He showed a deep solicitude for a risk in which, indeed, so much of his own reputation was practically invested. Letters exist which show his concern for the financial condition; he offered practical suggestions in regard to securing capital and placing stock; notwithstanding this desire to be of service among the friends of Brook Farm in New York, he, like others there, was then deeply immersed in the affairs at Red Bank, and was in no position to shoulder actual responsibility. It is evident that his main usefulness was confined to giving advice and to supplying moral fervor.

In two years more the tide of Fourierism had begun to ebb, and it carried out with it Brook Farm. But two vestiges were left on seemingly sure foundations, — the North American Phalanx, which lasted fourteen years, and of which

Greeley said "if it could not live, there was no hope for any other," and the Wisconsin, or Ceresco Phalanx. These too went soon. The assaults of some of the New York papers have already been mentioned. These secular papers were joined by the powerful *Observer*, which headed the outcry that the reform wished to "disorganize" society. The charge made against Fourier's views of sexual morality was damaging, and probably tended to injure Brook Farm to some extent. Even the American Union of Associationists, at their meeting of May, 1846, in Boston, felt constrained to protect themselves by asserting "*Fourierists* we are not and cannot consent to be called, because Fourier is only *one* of the great teachers of mankind."

Brisbane's own career as a doctrinaire properly closed with the ominous silence of Greeley and the ineluctable misadventure at West Roxbury. It is profitless to speculate as to whether too much system killed the Phalanx, or whether the simple cohesion of the first Association might have averted any serious trouble. There is little doubt, however, that Albert Brisbane, despite his lofty and disinterested character, proved to be the evil genius of Brook Farm.

LIST OF BOOKS AND MAGAZINE ARTICLES CITED OR USED

NOTE. — This list, though of reasonable fulness, is not offered as a complete bibliography.

ALCOTT, A. B. See Lane; Peabody; Sanborn.

ALCOTT, LOUISA MAY. Her Life, Letters, and Journals. Boston: Roberts Brothers, 1889. Especially the chapter on "Fruitlands," pp. 32–55. — Transcendental Wild Oats (in her Silver Pitchers).

ALEXANDER, J. W., and DOD, A. B. Two Articles from the Princeton Review concerning the Transcendental Philosophy of the Germans and of Cousin, and its Influence on Opinion in this Country. Cambridge: J. Owen, 1840.

ALHAIZA, A. Historique de l'École Sociétaire fondée par Fourier. Paris, 1894.

ALLEN, J. H. Our Liberal Movement in Theology. Boston: Roberts, 1882. — Sequel to Our Liberal Movement. Boston: Roberts Brothers, 1897.

Association as illustrated by Fourier's System. Printed for the American Union of Associationists. Boston, 1847.

BRADFORD, G. P. "Reminiscences of Brook Farm," by a Member of the Community. (In *Century Magazine*, 1892, Vol. 45, pp. 141–148.)

BRISBANE, A. A Concise Exposition of the Doctrine of Association. 2d ed. N. Y.: J. Redfield, 1843. — "On Association and Attractive Industry" [four papers]. (In *United States Magazine and Democratic Review*, 1842, New Series, Vol. 10.) —

"Sketch of his Life." (In *Same*, 1842, New Series, Vol. 11, pp. 302–305.) — Social Destiny of Man. Philadelphia, 1840.

BRISBANE, REDELIA. Albert Brisbane: A Mental Biography, by his Wife. Boston: Arena Publ. Co., 1893.

Brook Farm Association for Industry and Education. Constitution of the Brook Farm Association for Industry and Education, with an introductory Statement. 2d ed., with the By-laws. Boston, 1844.

Brook Farm Phalanx. The Community at West Roxbury, Mass. n.p. n.d. — Constitution, adopted May 1, 1845.

BROWNSON, O. A. "Brook Farm." (In *United States Magazine and Democratic Review*, 1842, New Series, Vol. 11, pp. 481–496.) — Charles Elwood, or the Infidel Converted. Boston: Little and Brown, 1840. — The Convert, or Leaves from My Experience. N. Y.: Dunigan, 1857. New edition, edited by H. F. Brownson, N. Y.: Sadlier & Co., 1877. — Essays and Reviews, chiefly on Theology, Politics, and Socialism. N. Y.: Sadlier & Co., 1852. — The Laboring Classes, an Article from the *Boston Quarterly Review*. Boston: B. H. Greene, 1840. — The Spirit Rapper, an Autobiography. Boston: Little, Brown, & Co., 1854.

BROWNSON, H. F. Orestes A. Brownson's Early Life, from 1803 to 1844. Detroit, 1898.

BURRAGE, H. S., editor. Brown University in the Civil War. Providence, 1868.

BURTON, W. The District School as it was. By one who went to it. Rev. ed. Boston: Phillips, Sampson, & Co., 1850. — Helps to Education in the Homes of Our Country. Boston: Crosby and Nichols, 1863. — My Religious Experience at my Native Home. Boston, 1832. — The Scenery Shower. Boston: W. D. Ticknor & Co., 1844.[1]

---

[1] Later editions were called "Scenery Showing."

CABOT, J. E. A Memoir of R. W. Emerson. Boston:
Houghton, Mifflin, & Co., 1887. 2 vols.

CARTER, R. "The 'Newness.'" (In *Century Magazine*,
1889, Vol. 39, pp. 124–131.) [1]

CARY, E. George William Curtis. Boston: Houghton,
Mifflin, & Co., 1894. [American Men of Letters.]

CHADWICK, J. W. George William Curtis. An Address.
New York: Harper, 1893. [Black and White Series.]
— Review of Codman's Brook Farm. (In *Nation*,
1895, Vol. 60, pp. 207–208.)

CHANNING, W. H. The Civil War in America. An ad-
dress. Liverpool [1861]. — "Ernest the Seeker." (In
Dial, July, October, 1840, Vol. 1, pp. 48–58, 233–
242). — A Statement of the Principles of the Christian
Union. New York, 1843. — Editor, Jouffroy, T. S.:
Introduction to Ethics. Translated by W. H. Chan-
ning. Boston, 1840. [Specimens of Foreign Standard
Literature.] — Editor, *The Present*. Vol. 1. New York,
1843–44.[2] — Editor, *The Spirit of the Age*. Vols. 1, 2,
July 7, 1849–April 27, 1850.[2] New York: Fowler &
Wells, 1850. See Frothingham; Fuller, Memoirs.

CHAPMAN, J. J. Emerson and Other Essays. New York:
Scribner, 1898.

CLARKE, J. F. Autobiography, Diary, and Correspon-
dence. Boston: Houghton, Mifflin, & Co., 1891.
— Memorial and Biographical Sketches. Boston:
Houghton, Osgood, & Co., 1878.

CODMAN, J. T. Brook Farm: Historic and Personal
Memoirs. Boston: Arena Publishing Company, 1894.
— "The Brook Farm Association." (In *Coming Age*,
1899, Vol. 2, pp. 33–38.) — "The Men and Thought
that Made the Boston of the Forties Famous." (In
Coming Age, 1899, Vol. 2, pp. 241–247.)

---

[1] There is a note by George S. Burleigh on p. 637 of the same volume relative to this paper.

[2] No more was issued.

COOKE, G. W. "Brook Farm." (In *New England Magazine*, 1897, Vol. 23, pp. 391–407.) — John Sullivan Dwight, Brook-Farmer, Editor, and Critic of Music. Boston: Small, Maynard, & Co., 1898. — Ralph Waldo Emerson: His Life, Writings, and Philosophy. Boston: J. R. Osgood, 1881. See Curtis.

CURTIS, G. W. Early Letters to John S. Dwight, Brook Farm and Concord. Edited by G. W. Cooke. New York: Harper, 1898. — Francis George Shaw. (In Other Essays from the *Easy Chair*. New York, 1893.)[1] — From the *Easy Chair*. Series 1–3. New York: Harper and Bros., 1892–1894. 3 vols. — The Howadji in Syria. New York: Harper, 1852. — Nile Notes of a Howadji. [Anon.] New York: Harper, 1851.

DALL, CAROLINE WELLS. Margaret and Her Friends, or Ten Conversations with Margaret Fuller. Boston: Roberts Brothers, 1895. — Transcendentalism in New England. Boston, 1897.[2]

DANA, C. A. A Lecture on Association in Its Connection with Religion, March 7, 1844. Boston: B. H. Greene, 1844.

Dial, The: a Magazine for Literature, Philosophy, and Religion. Vols. 1–4. Boston and London, 1841–44.

DOWDEN, E. "The Transcendental Movement and Literature." (In *Contemporary Review*, 1877, Vol. 33, pp. 297–318.)

DWIGHT, J. S. A Lecture on Association in its Connection with Education. Boston: B. H. Greene, 1844. — "Music a Means of Culture." (In *Atlantic Monthly*, 1870, Vol. 26, pp. 321–331.) — Editor, *Dwight's Journal of Music*. Vols. 1–41. Boston, 1853–1881. — Select Minor Poems, Translated from the German

---

[1] First appeared in *Harper's Magazine* for January, 1883, p. 306.

[2] Reprinted from the *Journal of Speculative Philosophy*, Vol. 23, No. 1.

of Goethe and Schiller. With notes by John S. Dwight. Boston: Hilliard, Gray, & Co., 1839. [Specimens of Foreign Standard Literature.] See Cooke; Curtis.

ELIOT, George. Margaret Fuller. (In her Essays and Reviews. Boston, 1887.)

ELLIOTT, W. The Life of Father Hecker. New York: Columbus Press, 1891.

ELLIS, C. M. An Essay on Transcendentalism. [Anon.] Boston: Crocker and Ruggles, 1842.

EMERSON, E. W. Emerson in Concord. Boston: Houghton, Mifflin, and Co., 1889.

EMERSON, R. W. "Fourierism and the Socialists." (In *Dial*, 1842, Vol. 3, pp. 86–89.) [1] — "Chardon Street and Bible Conventions." (In *Dial*, 1842, Vol. 3, pp. 100–112.) — "English Reformers." (In *Dial*, October, 1842, Vol. 3, pp. 227–247.) [2] — "Historic Notes of Life and Letters in Massachusetts." (In *Atlantic Monthly*, 1883, Vol. 53, pp. 529–543; also in his Lectures and Biographical Sketches, 1884, pp. 338–347.) — "Lectures on the Times. Lecture III. The Transcendentalist." (In *Dial*, 1843, Vol. 3, pp. 297–313.) — "Man the Reformer." (In *Dial*, 1841, Vol. 1, pp. 523–538.) — See Cabot; Chapman; Cooke; Fuller; Holmes; Sanborn.

FOURIER, F. M. C. Œuvres complètes. Paris, 1841–48, 6 v. — See Alhaiza; Association; Brisbane; Godwin; Harbinger; Pellarin; Phalanx; Warschauer.

FROTHINGHAM, O. B. George Ripley. Boston: Houghton, Mifflin, and Co., 1882. [American Men of Letters.] — Memoir of W. H. Channing. Boston: Houghton, Mifflin, and Co., 1886. — Recollections and Impres-

[1] This was introductory to an article by Albert Brisbane; the material was later used by Emerson in his Historic Notes, etc.

[2] Followed by a sketch of James Pierrepont Greaves, by Emerson, pp. 247–255, 281–296.

sions.   New York: G. P. Putnam's Sons, 1891. —
Theodore Parker: a Biography.   Boston: Osgood,
1874. — Transcendentalism in New England.   New
York: G. P. Putnam's Sons, 1876.

FULLER, Margaret, Marchesa d'Ossoli. Memoirs. Boston:
Phillips, Sampson, and Co., 1852.   2 Vols.[1] — See
Eliot, George; Higginson; Knortz.

GODWIN, Parke.   George William Curtis.   A Commemo-
rative Address before the Century Association, Dec.
17, 1892.   New York: Harper, 1893. — A Popular
View of the Doctrines of Charles Fourier.   New York:
Redfield, 1844.

GORDON, G. H.   Brook Farm to Cedar Mountain in the
War of the Great Rebellion.   Boston: Osgood and
Co., 1883.

GREELEY, H.   Hints toward Reforms.   New York:
Harper, 1850. — Recollections of a Busy Life.   New
York: J. B. Ford and Co., 1868. — See Ingersoll;
Parton; Sotheran; Zabriskie.

GREENE, W. B.   Transcendentalism.   West Brookfield,
Mass.: Press of Cooke and Co., 1849.

Harbinger, The, devoted to Social and Political Progress.
Vols. 1–4.   Published by the Brook Farm Phalanx.
New York: Burgess, Stringer, and Co.   Boston:
Redding and Co., 1845–47.   After Vol. 4 transferred
to the American Union of Associationists, and pub-
lished in New York till February, 1849.

HAWTHORNE, J.   Nathaniel Hawthorne and his Wife.
Boston: J. R. Osgood and Co., 1885. 2 vols.

HAWTHORNE, N.   The Blithedale Romance.   Boston:
Ticknor, Reed, and Fields, 1852. — Passages from
[his] American Note-books.   Boston: Ticknor and
Fields, 1868.   2 vols.

---

1 Vol. I., Youth; Cambridge, by J. F. Clarke; Groton and Providence, Concord, Boston, by R. W. Emerson.   Vol. II. Jamaica
Plain, by W. H. Channing; New York; Europe; Homeward. An
edition edited by A. B. Fuller was published in 1881.

HECKER, I. T. The Church and the Age. New York: The Catholic World, 1887. — Questions of the Soul. New York: Appleton, 1855. — "The Transcendental Movement in New England." (In *Catholic Review*, 1876, Vol. 23, pp. 528–537.) — See Elliott; Maignen.

HEDGE, F. H. [Coleridge's Literary Character.] (In *Christian Examiner*, 1833, Vol. 14, pp. 108–128.)

HIGGINSON, T. W. Cheerful Yesterdays. Houghton, Mifflin, & Co., 1898. — Margaret Ossoli Fuller. Boston: Houghton, Mifflin, & Co., 1884. [American Men of Letters.]

HOLMES, O. W. Ralph Waldo Emerson. Boston: Houghton, Mifflin, & Co., 1885. [American Men of Letters.]

HOWE, JULIA WARD. Margaret Fuller (Marchesa Ossoli). Boston: Roberts Brothers, 1883. [Famous Women.] Published also in London in the Eminent Women Series.

HUTCHINSON, J. W. Story of the Hutchinsons. Boston: Lee and Shepard, 1896. 2 vols.

INGERSOLL, L. D. The Life of Horace Greeley. Chicago, 1873.

KIRBY, GEORGIANNA (BRUCE). My First Visit to Brook Farm. [Anon.] [San Francisco, 1870].[1] — "Reminiscences of Brook Farm." (In *Old and New*, 1871, Vol. 3, pp. 425–438; Vol. 4, pp. 347–358. 1872, Vol. 5, pp. 517–530.) — Years of Experience. An Autobiographical Narrative. New York: G. P. Putnam's Sons, 1887.

KNORTZ, C. Brook Farm und Margaret Fuller. New York: Druck von H. Bartsch, 1886.

LANE, C. "A. Bronson Alcott's Works." (In *Dial*, 1843, Vol. 3, pp. 417–454).[2] — "Brook Farm." (In *Dial*,

[1] Reprinted from the *Overland Monthly*, Vol. 5.
[2] Reprinted as The Law and Method in Spirit Culture (Boston, 1843).

U

1844, Vol. 4, pp. 351–357). — "Social Tendencies." (In *Dial*, 1843, Vol. 4, pp. 65–86, 188–204.)

LINCOLN, W. S. Life with the Thirty-fourth Mass. Infantry in the War of the Rebellion. Worcester, 1879.

McGINLEY, A. A. "Brook Farm To-day." (In *Catholic World*, 1895, Vol. 61, pp. 14–25.)

MAIGNEN, CHARLES. Études sur l'Américanisme. Le Père Hecker, est-il un Saint? Rome: Desclée, Lefebvre et Cie, 1899.

MITCHELL, D. G. American Lands and Letters. New York, 1899. 2 vols.

"New England Reformers." (In *Atlantic Monthly*, 1884, Vol. 54, pp. 713–715.)

NEWCOMB, C. K. Dolon. (In *Dial*, 1842, Vol. 3, pp. 112–123.)

NORTON, A. A Discourse on the Latest Form of Infidelity. Cambridge: J. Owen, 1839. — Remarks on a Pamphlet [by George Ripley], entitled "The Latest Form of Infidelity examined." Cambridge: Owen, 1839.

ORR, J. "The Transcendentalism of New England." (In *International Review*, 1882, Vol. 13, pp. 381–398.)

ORVIS, J. A Plan for the Organization and Management of Coöperative Stores and Boards of Trade. Mechanicsburg: Sovereigns of Industry Bulletin print [1876.]

PARKER, T. A Discourse on the Transient and Permanent in Christianity, preached at the Ordination of C. C. Shackford, in Boston, May 19, 1841. Boston: printed for the author, 1841. — A Discourse of Matters pertaining to Religion. Boston: Little & Brown, 1842. — Transcendentalism. A Lecture. Boston: Free Religious Association, 1876. [Free Religious Tracts, No. 4]. See Frothingham; Weiss.

PARTON, JAMES. Life of Horace Greeley. New York: Mason, 1855. Same. Boston: Osgood, 1872.

PEABODY, ELIZABETH P. "Fourierism." (In *Dial*, 1844, Vol. 4, pp. 473-483). — "A Glimpse of Christ's Idea of Society." (In *Dial*, 1841, Vol. 2, pp. 214-228). — Last Evening with Allston, and Other Papers. Boston: D. Lothrop & Co. [1886.] — "Plan of the West Roxbury Community." (In *Dial*, 1842, Vol. 2, pp. 361-372.)

PELLARIN, C. Life of Charles Fourier. 2d ed. Translated by F. G. Shaw. N. Y.: Graham, 1848.

Phalanx, The. A Journal of Social Science. (Vol. 1, Nos. 1-23.) New York, 1843-45.[1]

RIPLEY, GEORGE. "Brownson's Writings." (In *Dial*, 1840, Vol. 1, pp. 22-46.) — Defence of "The Latest Form of Infidelity" examined. A second letter to Andrews Norton. Boston: Munroe & Co. — A Farewell Discourse delivered to the Congregational Church in Purchase Street, March 28, 1841. Boston, 1841. — "Henry Pestalozzi and His Plan of Education." (In *Christian Examiner*, 1831, Vol. 11, pp. 347-373.) — "The Latest Forms of Infidelity" examined. A letter to Andrews Norton. Boston: Munroe, 1839. — Letter addressed to the Congregational Church in Purchase Street, by its pastor. Boston, 1840. — A Third Letter to Andrews Norton. Boston: Munroe, 1840. Editor, Specimens of Foreign Standard Literature. Boston, 1838-42. 14 vols. See Frothingham.

Roxbury, Mass. Report of the Joint Special Committee on the Removal of the Almshouse and the Purchase of Brook Farm. Roxbury: J. G. Torrey, City printer, 1849.

RUSSELL, AMELIA. "Home Life of the Brook Farm Association." (In *Atlantic Monthly*, 1878, Vol. 42, pp. 458-466, 556-563.)

SALISBURY, ANNIE MARIA. Brook Farm. [Marlborough, Mass.: Smith, 1898.]

---

[1] Continued by the *Harbinger*.

SANBORN, F. B., editor. The Genius and Character of Emerson. Lectures at the Concord School of Philosophy. [In 1884.] Boston: Osgood, 1885.

SANBORN, F. B., and HARRIS, W. T. A. Bronson Alcott: His Life and Philosophy. Boston: Roberts Brothers, 1893. 2 vols.

SAXTON, J. A. Prophecy — Transcendentalism — Progress. (In *Dial*, 1841, Vol. 2, pp. 83–121.)

SHAW, F. G. See Curtis; Pellarin.

SOTHERAN, C. Horace Greeley and Other Pioneers of American Socialism. New York [1892].

SUMNER, A. "A Boy's Recollections of Brook Farm." (In *New England Magazine*, 1894, Vol. 16, pp. 309–313.)

TARBELL, A. W. "The Brook Farm Experiment." Illustrated. (In *National Magazine*, 1897, Vol. 7, pp. 195–203.)

TIFFANY, F. "Transcendentalism: the New England Renaissance." (In *Unitarian Review*, 1889, Vol. 31, pp. 97–117.)

WALL, ANNIE. "Early Transcendentalism in New England." (In *New England Magazine*, 1886, Vol. 5, pp. 162–170.)

WARSCHAUER, O. Geschichte des Socialismus und Kommunismus im 19. Jahrhundert. Abt. 1–3. Leipzig, 1892–96.

WEISS, J. Life and Correspondence of Theodore Parker. New York: Appleton, 1864. 2 vols.

WINTER, W. George William Curtis. A Eulogy. New York: Macmillan, 1893.

ZABRISKIE, F. N. Horace Greeley, the Editor. New York: Funk & Wagnalls, 1890.

INDEX

Acting at Brook Farm, 60.

Admiral, The. See Blake.

Aerie. See Eyrie.

Agricultural implements, 42.

Agriculture, instruction in, 70.

Albert Edward, Prince of Wales, 223.

Alcott, A. Bronson, 7, 9, 49, 57, 59, 88, 101, 206, 233–241, 260.

Alcott House School, 238.

Alexander, J. W., 13.

Alist, 238.

Allen, Mrs. J. T. See Kittredge, C. A.

Allen, Rev. John, 117, 148, 176, 181–184, 268, 278; his son attacked by smallpox, 182, 183.

Allen, Rev. Joseph H., 247.

Allen, William B., 18, 19, 22, 134, 167.

Alvord, Anna G., 26, 31, 32.

Ambition, defended by Dana, 148.

"American Cyclopædia," 138.

American Union of Associationists, 265, 281.

Americanism in the Roman Catholic Church, 109.

Amusement Group, 60, 127.

Amusements at Brook Farm, 53–68.

Andrews, Stephen Pearl, 268.

Anthon, Charles, 147.

Antislavery, 63, 64, 113, 122, 182, 256.

Applicants for admission, 112, 113, 133.

Archon, nickname for Ripley, 133.

Articles of Association, 17, 20, 21.

Associates. See Members.

Association, 12, 276, 279; defended by Dana, 147, 148; *Harbinger* devoted to, 263, 265.

Association of the Evangelical Lutheran Church for Works of Mercy, 26.

Associationist meetings, 63, 147, 154, 222.

Atlantic Monthly, 126.

"Attica," 28.

Baking at Brook Farm, 52, 97, 98, 120.

Baldwin, Peter ("The General"), 28, 49, 52, 56, 61, 120, 121.

Bancroft, George, 4, 8, 144.

Bancroft, George and John, pupils, 72.

Barham, F., 238.

Barlow, Mrs. Almira, 27, 80, 127, 128, 173.

Barlow, General F. C., 82, 83, 256.

Barmby, Goodwyn, 238.

Barn, 29.

Barrett, Nathan, 89.

Bartlett, Robert, 7.

Bartol, Rev. Cyrus A., 7.

Beethoven, 156.

Belles-lettres, taught by Bradford, 74.

Biscaccianti, Signora, 61, 164.

Blake, Thomas ("The Admiral"), 28, 121.

"Blithedale Romance" (Hawthorne's), 165, 167, 169, 171, 172.

Board of Direction, 113.

Boating at Brook Farm, 77, 81.

Boisterousness lacking in pupils, 71.

Boston, 44, 259, 269; transcendentalism in, 1, 3; music in, 63, 156; Ripley's chapter on "Philosophic Thought in," 144, 193; visits to, 55,

THREE STUDIES IN LITERATURE.

BY

LEWIS EDWARDS GATES,
Assistant Professor of English in Harvard University.

Cloth. 12mo. $1.50.

FRANCIS JEFFREY.
CARDINAL NEWMAN.
MATTHEW ARNOLD.

ASPECTS OF THE
ROMANTIC PERIOD OF
ENGLISH LITERATURE.

"Professor Gates is fortunate in his subjects; his subjects are fortunate in his justly discriminating appreciation. The reader is fortunate in his illuminating treatment of these notable characters, often misunderstood and disparaged, — the brilliant reviewer, the spiritual rhetorician, the humanistic critic. These masterly Studies should be in the hands of all students of our literature in this century."

—*Outlook.*

THE MACMILLAN COMPANY,

66 FIFTH AVENUE, NEW YORK.

NATIONAL STUDIES IN AMERI-CAN LETTERS

Old Cambridge

BY

THOMAS WENTWORTH HIGGINSON

Cloth. 12mo. Price $1.25

" . . . Some charmingly reminiscent pages, having for their subject the three authors most widely associated with Old Cambridge, — Holmes, Longfellow, and Lowell; and their pleasant gossip makes up the major part of the volume, which is altogether a most enjoyable and valuable one." — *Philadelphia Evening Telegraph.*

" It is just the sort of book that one would expect from the author, graceful in form, abounding in the genuine atmosphere of the old university town, full of pleasant personal anecdotes and reminiscences of the Cambridge of forty or fifty years ago. Many great figures pass across the stage, with nearly all of whom Colonel Higginson was personally acquainted; and this intimacy gives the book a charming flavor." — *Brooklyn Life.*

" The book contains material to be had nowhere else, for it is a commentary on the side history of a great epoch in American letters, written by one who had a place in it." — *San Francisco Argonaut.*

" What he has to tell will be interesting to every person who honors New England and sets store by her literature. The book is steeped in the Attic dew of which the Cambridge cicadas were fond; it has a smack of ambrosia, — American ambrosia, — and its leaves rustle with the unmistakable Parnassian suggestion — a Puritan Parnassus to be sure. . . . The Cambridge he dwells upon is the Cambridge of the Boston circle of poets, philosophers, politicians, reformers, scholars, statesmen, preachers, and divine cranks. He sketches everything and everybody freely, swiftly, and lightly." — *Independent.*

THE MACMILLAN COMPANY
66 FIFTH AVENUE, NEW YORK